Understanding Jesus Today

JESUS' CALL TO DISCIPLESHIP

Understanding Jesus Today

Edited by Howard Clark Kee

Growing interest in the historical Jesus can be frustrated by diverse and conflicting claims about what he said and did. This series brings together in accessible form the conclusions of an international team of distinguished scholars regarding various important aspects of Jesus' teaching. All of the authors have extensively analyzed the biblical and contextual evidence about who Jesus was and what he taught, and they summarize their findings here in easily readable and stimulating discussions. Each book includes an appendix of questions for further thought and recommendations for further reading on the topic covered.

Other Books in the Series

Howard Clark Kee, *What Can We Know About Jesus?*
Pheme Perkins, *Jesus as Teacher*
David Tiede, *Jesus and the Future*
John Riches, *The World of Jesus: First-Century Judaism in Crisis*

Jesus' Call to Discipleship

JAMES D. G. DUNN

CAMBRIDGE
UNIVERSITY PRESS

Published by the Press Syndicate of the University of Cambridge
The Pitt Building, Trumpington Street, Cambridge CB2 1RP
40 West 20th Street, New York, NY 10011-4211, USA
10 Stamford Road, Oakleigh, Victoria 3166, Australia

First published 1992

Printed in the United States of America

Library of Congress Cataloging-in-Publication Data
Dunn, James D. G., 1939–
Jesus' call to discipleship / James D. G. Dunn.
    p.   cm.
Includes bibliographical references and index.
ISBN 0–521–41434–2 (hard). – ISBN 0–521–42481–X (pbk.)
1. Jesus Christ – Teachings.   2. Kingdom of God – Biblical
teaching.
3. Christian life – Biblical teaching.   4. Church – Biblical
teaching.
5. Bible. N.T. Gospels – Criticism, interpretation, etc.
I. Title.
BS2417.K5D86   1992
232.9'54–dc20   91–39842
                                                          CIP
A catalog record for this book is available from the British Library.

ISBN 0–521–41434–2 hardback
ISBN 0–521–42481–X paperback

To the memory of
J. W. Meiklejohn, M.B.E.
(1910–1989)

known to generations of
Scripture Union in Scotland as
"The Boss"

who called many to the
discipleship of the Jesus
he served so faithfully.

Contents

Preface   *page* ix

1   Introduction   1
2   The Call of the Kingdom   6
3   Good News for the Poor   32
4   The Boundary Breaker   62
5   Would Jesus Have Been Disappointed
    with the Church?   92
6   Concluding Reflections   121

Selected Bibliography   129
Questions for Discussion   131
Index   135

Preface

These chapters began life as a series of four public lectures delivered in November 1987 on the theme of "Jesus and Discipleship" for the Durham Council of Churches. By that time I was already committed to contributing on the same theme to the *Understanding Jesus Today* series, and it seemed wisest to use the lectures as a first draft (as it were) for the book. The constraints of the lecture format were thus a major factor in determining the content and order of the material.

When it came to writing up the lectures (delivered from notes), the temptation to break out of the four-lecture/chapter format was considerable, but the lectures had been well received and proved pleasingly coherent, and I had promised that they would be published. I therefore stayed with the four-chapter format (with the addition of an introduction and conclusion), since any ordering of such material is bound to be artificial in one degree or another.

In view of the nature of the subject I have not hesitated to pose questions for discussion that go beyond issues of merely historical interest.

I wish to express my gratitude to the Durham Council for the invitation to give the lectures and to the original audiences for the feedback and stimulus which the open discussion period following each lecture contributed to the subsequent write-up.

Chapter 1

Introduction

The Challenge

In the history of humankind there are few men or women who have had more influence than Jesus. He obviously made a profound impact on many of those he met. We need not enter the long-running debates as to whether he was a man just like any other man, or was unique in unique degree. The fact is that he must have been a person of no little power and personal magnetism. Of no one else has it been said so often down through the centuries, "Would it not have been wonderful to see him for ourselves, to hear his own voice, to spend time with him." And understandably so: An encounter with Jesus evidently proved for many of his contemporaries to be a life-transforming experience. Their lives became oriented round him, as the one who gave it center and focus. And the combined impact was sufficient to launch a movement which became in due course a religion of world importance, shaping the history of nations and the culture of continents.

Discipleship of Jesus, then, is a topic of tremendous interest in itself. Not only is it about following this Jesus, what following him meant. But it is also about those who followed – men and women who in turn have left a very substantial mark on the history of the world in what they accomplished and in the church they launched. And since they put their success down to their discipleship of Jesus, perhaps their discipleship is the key to their success. To inquire, then, what discipleship meant in practice, what following him actually involved, may have a wider significance for any interested in the secret of what it is in human relationships that moves minds and hearts and transforms lives.

The topic should be of particular interest to those who already in some sense or other think of themselves as disciples of Jesus. For, any understanding of what discipleship of Jesus is and involves must surely take its lead from the discipleship to which he actually called followers during his life and ministry. Of course, discipleship in the twentieth century cannot be a mere imitation of discipleship in first-century Galilee. That would be playacting at discipleship, motivated by a morbid fascination with first-century trappings rather than by a sincere desire to share the spirit which motivated the first disciples. But discipleship of Jesus must nonetheless draw its understanding of that discipleship from the record of those who literally followed him, otherwise such claims to discipleship can easily become fanciful and subject to distorting pressures from tradition and ecclesiastical vested interest.

The same point can be expressed in more weighty theological terms. In Jesus, Christians believe they have seen the incarnation of God, God showing human creatures what God is like in personal, human terms. In the purpose of God it was evidently necessary to go beyond the words given through inspiration to priest and prophet, to lawgiver, sage and psalmist. It was evidently necessary for God to make himself vulnerable to the processes of history, and his revelation vulnerable to the historical encounter of person with person. The incarnation was the high point of God's self-revelation. All other claims to understand God and the will of God have to be read in its light. As far as Christians are concerned, all other such claims have to be brought to the touchstone of the historical revelation of God in Christ.

And this must include the claim to understand what discipleship means or should mean now or in the future. For the

Christian and/or would-be disciple of Jesus, therefore, it is essential to scrutinize the records of the original discipleship of Jesus, in order to gain insight into the spirit and character of that discipleship, in order to get some kind of yardstick by which to measure one's own discipleship.

The Task

But how much can we learn of the actual discipleship of Jesus? Jesus himself left no manual of discipleship behind him. We have four Gospels, which appear to be written by some of Jesus' first disciples or their immediate associates. But they do not set out to provide manuals of discipleship either. And most people interested in the subject will be aware that their historical value is a matter of considerable debate. Many scholars who have made a special study of the Gospels doubt whether all the sayings attributed to Jesus in the Gospels go back to him. So the question inevitably arises: Can we gain a sufficiently clear picture of the discipleship for which Jesus called?

To this particular question, however, a fairly confident answer, "Yes," can be given. There is a strong probability anyway that the bulk of the traditions in at least the first three Gospels consists of the earliest memories of what Jesus did and said. As we might expect, many of the episodes show evidence of repeated retellings, and many of the sayings and parables show evidence of frequent re-usage. On the one hand, that means stories have been elaborated to speak with greater appeal to different audiences, sayings have been interpreted, with explanations added, to make them clearer and to give them sharper application to subsequent situations. But on the other hand, that same evidence indicates a desire to remember and repeat and re-use these earliest memories. The initial impact on original spectators or hearers was such that some of them had wanted to resavor it in relating it to others. And for the group of

Jesus' disciples these stories and sayings had a crucial importance, since the stories explained (to themselves and others) why they had become members of the group, why the group existed in the first place. The elaboration and interpretation added to the traditions was a way of translating the original impact of the event or saying it to a different audience. In other words, in, with, and through such elaboration and interpretation we have fuller evidence of the impact of the original version.

And this will be particularly true of the discipleship material. For, the events and sayings of Jesus' ministry which called them to discipleship, which shaped the character of their discipleship, or which provided the model for their discipleship will have been among the Jesus traditions which the first disciples were most eager to preserve and pass on. What had called them to discipleship they would hope would work in the same way with others. What had been the greatest stimulus and challenge to their discipleship they would want to keep for their own continuing use and benefit, as well as for others'.

This would continue to be the case in some measure as the circle of discipleship broadened. It is true that the call to discipleship in the early churches was a call to faith in the risen Christ, rather than simply a repeating of the message of Jesus. But the character of that discipleship, as expressed in the attitudes and motivations which governed everyday life, was still more clearly encapsulated in the character of the Jesus traditions than anywhere else. And the form of these traditions was probably already well established in the church at Jerusalem before the major expansion beyond Palestine got under way. Moreover, those who professed discipleship of a Jesus whom they had never seen would almost certainly cherish the accounts of those who had first followed Jesus in Galilee, as an indication to themselves and to others of what such discipleship of the risen Christ still involved.

We can therefore enter upon our task with some confidence. Every so often we shall have to take account of the issue of a key saying's historical value and significance. But for the most part the testimony and the trend of the evidence are consistent and sufficiently strong for us to take them more or less at face value. Of course there will be several points where different scholars would read the evidence differently. But the overall picture which emerges in the following chapters is so clear across the different traditions, and mutually coherent at so many different points in the several traditions, that it is unlikely to suffer more than a few dents.

We will start with the feature of Jesus' message which seems to have been most characteristic of his message and most memorable as such – his proclamation of the Kingdom of God (Chapter 2). In Chapters 3 and 4 we will focus our attention on the question, To whom was Jesus' call to discipleship primarily directed, and what does this tell us about the character of the discipleship to which he called? In Chapter 5 we ask after the communal character of the discipleship of Jesus and attempt to sketch its main features. A final brief conclusion draws together some of the most challenging aspects of the discipleship of Jesus for potential, would-be, and professed disciples today.

Chapter 2

The Call of the Kingdom

Now after John was arrested, Jesus came into Galilee, preaching the Gospel of God, and saying, "The time is fulfilled, and the Kingdom of God is at hand: Repent, and believe in the Gospel. (Mark 1:14–15)

Introduction

What was it that caught people's attention with regard to Jesus? According to our Gospels crowds gathered to listen to him. Why did they come? What was it that attracted people to Jesus? According to our Gospels many followed him. Why should they do that?

An important part of the answer must lie in Jesus' message of the Kingdom. Talk of the Kingdom was evidently one of the most striking and consistent features of his preaching. In the quotation at the head of the chapter Mark sums up Jesus' message in terms of "the Kingdom of God" (to avoid speaking of God so directly Matthew prefers the phrase "Kingdom of Heaven," but the meaning is the same). When Jesus later sent out his disciples in mission he focused their message in the same words – "The Kingdom of Heaven is at hand" (Matt. 10:7; Luke 10:9). It is generally recognized that parables were Jesus' most distinctive method of teaching; and his most frequent category of parables regularly begins with the words, "The Kingdom (of Heaven) is like . . . " (Matt. 13:24, 31, 33, 44, 45, 47; etc.). In Mark, which does not contain so much of Jesus' teaching, the phrase occurs thirteen times. Matthew has another thirty-six references, and Luke another eighteen. So Jesus' emphasis on the Kingdom was obviously one of the most memorable aspects of his ministry.

Jesus' audiences, of course, would be familiar with the thought of God as king. They would address him as king regularly in their worship – as, often, in the psalms. For example,

> Lift up your heads, O gates!
>   and be lifted up, O ancient doors!
>   that the King of glory may come in.
> Who is the King of glory?
>   The Lord, strong and mighty,
>   the Lord, mighty in battle!
> Lift up your heads, O gates!
>   and be lifted up, O ancient doors!
>   that the King of glory may come in.
> Who is this King of glory?
>   The Lord of hosts,
>   he is the King of glory. (Ps. 24:7–10)

In Dan. 4:34 the prayer of Nebuchadnezzar expresses recognition of the truth of Israel's faith. He

blessed the Most High, and praised and honoured him who lives for ever:

> for his dominion is an everlasting dominion,
> and his kingdom endures from generation to generation.

And in a very old prayer, which probably goes back to the time of Jesus (the Kaddish) Jesus and his contemporaries would have prayed, "May he (God) establish his Kingdom in your lifetime and in your days, and in the lifetime of the whole house of Israel, speedily and at a near time."

Even so, talk of the Kingdom appears much less frequently in our Jewish sources from this period than it does in the first three Gospels. Jesus evidently made it a central feature of his message in a way that no one else had been doing. He brought Jewish faith and prayer to focus on the Kingdom of God as no one else had. He took seriously God's kingship, as a factor which could not be ignored, with a forcefulness that lived in the memory of his disciples.

More striking still was his vivid use of the phrase. Jesus' hearers would have found the phrase itself familiar enough. But Jesus spoke of the Kingdom "at hand" (Mark 1:15); of the Kingdom being "violently treated" (Matt. 11:12); of the Kingdom having "come upon" people (Luke 11:20); of "entering into the Kingdom" (Mark 10:23–5); of "receiving" the Kingdom (Mark 10:15); and of the Kingdom "coming" (Luke 11:2). Such a variety of metaphor is without parallel at the time of Jesus. Clearly the phrase on Jesus' lips was no wooden stereotype or a mouthing of traditional platitudes. There was something dynamic, even startling in his usage. Even a Jew long familiar with the thought of God as king must have quickly realized that this phrase in Jesus' teaching was altogether more important than he had hitherto appreciated, altogether more compelling of his attention.

One other point should be borne in mind: that the first Christians do not seem to have used the phrase very much either. The frequency of usage we find in, for example, Acts and the letters of Paul is more like the relative infrequency in contemporary Judaism than its prominence in the first three Gospels. This makes the testimony of the Gospels all the more striking. Despite the fact that they did not themselves speak much of God's Kingdom, the first Christians nevertheless remembered that Jesus had done so. They remembered that God's kingship was one of his main emphases, and cherished the traditions which now make up our first three Gospels. In other words, these Gospels continue to reflect the distinctiveness of Jesus' preaching on this point. And the fact that they have retained that emphasis in their own formulation is itself a continuing expression of the impact Jesus' teaching made.

So we can give a first answer to our opening questions. One

of the features of Jesus' ministry which caused people to sit up
and take notice was *his message of the Kingdom of God*. Others had talked and did talk about God as king; but the emphasis
Jesus put upon God's kingship marked his teaching out and
formed a distinctive and striking feature of Jesus' ministry.
This was one aspect of Jesus' proclamation which obviously
attracted potential disciples and which continued to live in the
memory of those who followed.

Why so? Thus far we have hardly moved beyond bare statistics. Can we penetrate further? What was it about Jesus' message of the Kingdom that proved such an attraction? What was
it in his mission that turned hearers into disciples?

"The Kingdom of God . . . "

What Was He Talking About?

We have a problem at once with translation. The problem is
that our word "kingdom" is too static. It fits well enough into
some of the range of Jesus' usage illustrated above, particularly
his talk of "entering into the Kingdom" (e.g., Matt. 18:3; Mark
9:47), and of "sitting down" (as in Matt. 8:11 and 20:21). But
Jesus' imagery was much more extensive. He likens the Kingdom to seeds growing (Mark 4:26–9), or to leaven in a lump of
dough (Luke 13:20), or to unexpected finds of immense value
(Matt. 13:44–6). Here the imagery of a territory ruled over by a
king (like the United Kingdom) seems to be less appropriate.

The problem, however, is primarily one of translation. In the
original language Jesus used (Aramaic) the word which has
been translated "kingdom" is itself broader. It is a much more
dynamic concept. More central to its meaning is the idea of the
rule exercised by a king. That includes, by extension, the
thought of the area over which such rule is exercised. But it is
the idea of rule being exercised which we lose in the transla-

tion "kingdom." And it is that which we need to preserve in order to appreciate the full scope of Jesus' usage. In particular, it is important to realize that in Aramaic versions of the Old Testament "the Kingdom of God" was equivalent to God himself in the exercise of his sovereignty. All this means that we really need a different translation than "kingdom," and explains why most New Testament scholars prefer to speak of God's "rule" or God's "reign."

If we want to gain a better understanding of the impact of Jesus' preaching about the Kingdom of God, therefore, we need to grasp two important points at once. (1) By his talk of the "Kingdom" Jesus meant something *dynamic*, the exercise of royal power and authority. The image of a territory over which the king reigns is only part of the whole picture. What Jesus had in mind was much more the practical out-working and effect of kingly rule. (2) More important, Jesus always spoke of the kingly rule *of God* (Matthew's "of Heaven" comes to the same thing). When he spoke of God's Kingdom there was no thought whatsoever of a territory where the king's rule was merely nominal (absentee landlord). Precisely the opposite. What he was actually talking about was God's effective rule, God acting as king.

This makes better sense of the range of Jesus' imagery reviewed above. God's rule can be accepted ("entered into"), enjoyed ("feast in"), is invisible in the wonder of life and growth, can be discovered unexpectedly as of inestimable value, and so on. It was at least partly because Jesus was taking a familiar thought (God's rule) and making so much of it and expressing it in such vigorous metaphors that his talk of the Kingdom was so memorable. Here was something, God's reign, which had become too much taken for granted, spoken of in too-familiar terms. Jesus' vigorous message made it a much more vivid and pressing reality, something which demanded their attention and response in a new way.

"The Time is Fulfilled"

But there is more to be said. It was not just the vivid way Jesus spoke of the Kingdom that must have caught his hearers' attention. His contemporaries would have had no difficulty in the thought of God as reigning, or indeed of the kingdom of Israel as the expression of God's reign. But the way Jesus spoke of God's Kingdom was different. He claimed that God's kingly rule was especially active in and through his own ministry. They also looked for a fuller manifestation of that kingly rule some time in the future, when, in terms of Daniel's visions, the stone "cut out by no human hand . . . became a great mountain and filled the whole earth," and "the saints of the Most High" were given "the kingdom and the dominion and the greatness of the kingdoms under the whole heaven" (Dan. 2:34–5; 7:27). But Jesus clearly implied that this final rule of God was *already* coming to expression in his own ministry.

His own teaching spoke of this particularly in relation to two important aspects of his ministry. The first was *exorcisms*, which were evidently quite a prominent part of his ministry, whether they are to be understood as (or included) only the restoration of the psychologically maladjusted or as also the liberating of some who had been spiritually crippled. Here again, exorcism was nothing new to his audiences (Matt. 12:27; Mark 9:38). But Jesus saw his exorcisms, achieved by the immediate power of God, as an expression of the rule of God, and so also as an indication that Satan's rule was already broken (Matt. 12:28; Mark 3:27) – something expected by his contemporaries only in the last day (as in Isa. 24:21–2). There was a healing and restoration and liberation taking place in and through his ministry which had been a hope cherished only for the age to come (Matt. 11:5, referring to Isa. 29:18, 35:5–6, and 61:1).

Secondly, he saw his practice of *table-fellowship* in the same light. For Jesus it already mirrored the character of the festal banquet of the new age (e.g., Mark 2:18–19; Luke 14:12–24), again using imagery which his contemporaries would relate primarily to the hoped-for future (as in Isa. 25:6–9). The metaphor of the wedding feast was an obvious one to depict the contrast between lives lived normally at subsistence level and the fuller life of God's Kingdom to come. But Jesus saw the sharing of food in common round the meal table in openness and acceptance as already expressing the character of the great celebration to come in God's Kingdom.

This latter feature of Jesus' ministry is one to which we will have to return. For the moment our question is simply, What was it about Jesus' message of God's kingly rule that made it so memorable among those attracted to him? And the answer is clear. Jesus came not simply with a message of future hope; rather, it was a message lived out before their eyes. What previously could only be hoped for was now beginning to happen. What many prophets and righteous had longed to see and hear was now being seen and heard by those drawn into his circle (Matt. 13:16–17).

To sum up thus far, then, we can say that Jesus' message about the Kingdom of God would have caught attention for several reasons. (1) He made the message of God's rule *central* to his preaching in a way that made him stand out from his contemporaries. (2) He spoke of God's rule in a way which made it impossible for those who attended to what he said to ignore that rule or effectively to push it to the margins of their lives. (3) He lived and acted in a way which showed that God's final triumph need not be thought of merely as a starry-eyed hope but was *already a power evident in his own ministry,* not least in the healing of demoniacs and in the acceptance of his meal table.

What did this mean for discipleship? To those "caught" by

this message it meant at least two things: a readiness to acknowledge the importance of the rule of God as a factor in daily
living and as a fact of enormous power; and the recognition
that Jesus' ministry provided a window into that rule and a
means of relating more directly and positively to it. But this is
only the beginning of the answer.

". . . Is at Hand"

A Fundamental Issue

So far we have simply noted the vivid quality of Jesus' talk of
the Kingdom and the powerful attraction his lived-out message
of the Kingdom must have exerted for many who saw and
heard him. But there was a whole further dimension of his
preaching we have not yet touched on – the *gravity* of his
message. It was never the case that Jesus spoke of the Kingdom
in a take-it-or-leave-it way, as though it did not matter how his
hearers responded. He was no mere rhetorician, self-indulgent
in the vigor of his metaphors, content simply to delight and
dazzle. Quite the contrary! His message was about fundamental issues, matters of life and death. How his hearers responded
would determine how their whole lives were built and what
their final outcome would be.

> Do not fear those who kill the body
>   but cannot kill the soul;
> rather fear him who can destroy
>   both soul and body in hell. (Matt. 10:28)
>
> And if your hand or your foot causes you to sin,
>   cut it off and throw it away;
> it is better for you to enter life maimed or lame
>   than with two hands or two feet
>   to be thrown into the eternal fire. (Matt. 18:8)
>
> Everyone who hears these words of mine and does them
>   will be like a wise man who built his house upon the rock;

and the rain fell, and the floods came,
    and the winds blew and beat upon that house,
but it did not fall,
    because it had been founded on the rock.
And everyone who hears these words of mine and does not do
    them
    will be like a foolish man who built his house upon the
    sand;
and the rain fell, and the floods came,
    and the winds blew and beat against that house,
and it fell;
    and great was the fall of it. (Matt. 7:24–7)

Everyone who acknowledges me before men,
    the Son of Man will also acknowledge before the angels of
    God;
but he who denies me before men
    will be denied before the angels of God. (Luke 12:8–9)

If we take such words seriously, as many obviously did, we
can begin to see just how fundamental were the issues which
were bound up for Jesus in his proclamation of God's kingly
rule. This incidentally is why it is so difficult to portray Jesus
well in plays and films. There was a seriousness about his
message which permitted no easy or flippant response. Yet, at
the same time, he was no killjoy or long-faced preacher of
doom. "A glutton and drunkard" they called him, in contrast to
John the Baptist (Matt. 11:19). His lived-out message of the
table-fellowship of the Kingdom put feasting before fasting
(Mark 2:19). But all that did not make the seriousness of the
issues with which he confronted his hearers and the gravity of
the response for which he called any the less.

An Urgent Call

The call was not only serious, but *urgent*. "God's Kingdom has
drawn near; God's rule is at hand" (Mark 1:15). For all that
Jesus' ministry brought God's kingly rule to expression, a full-

er, and final manifestation of God's sovereign authority was waiting to be unleashed. Were they ready for it? To assume that, because God's final reign had delayed already for centuries, it was of no pressing importance, could be fatal. The fact that the final rule of God was already coming to expression in Jesus' ministry was not a reason to relax but rather to increase vigilance.

So with Jesus' call to discipleship: To one man he said, "Follow me." The man responded, "Lord, let me first go and bury my father." But Jesus told him, "Leave the dead to bury their own dead; but as for you, go and proclaim the Kingdom of God" (Luke 9:59–60). The offensiveness of Jesus' reply would be difficult to match. To bury his father was one of the most elementary duties of a son; in Jewish custom it came before other fundamental religious responsibilities (like reciting the Shema). But Jesus saw the response of the man as an attempt to diminish the importance of the call to discipleship, as an excuse to lessen the urgency of its claim upon him. Similarly with the other episode which Luke adds in at this point.

Another said, "I will follow you, Lord; but let me first say farewell to those at my home." Jesus said to him, "No one who puts his hand to the plough and looks back is fit for the Kingdom of God." (Luke 9:61–2)

Notice once again the same sense of urgency: There is no time for the would-be disciple even to say farewell to his family.

A similar note of urgency is present in Luke's second version of the disciples' commission: "Exchange no greetings on the road" (Luke 10:4). This too would be very offensive. In the Middle East greetings have a deeper significance than in the West, not least because the religious language used would be taken seriously. In Jesus' time they probably involved some element of ceremony and consumed some time. The messengers of the Kingdom do not have that time. Their message is urgent, and must be given first priority.

When we link this back into what has already been said about Jesus' sense of God's kingly rule coming already to expression in and through his ministry (in word and deed), the point becomes clear. Jesus calls for his audience to open their eyes to reality. Wake up to what is already happening! It was all too possible to be so absorbed in one's own affairs and with social or religious proprieties as to fail to recognize God already at work – like the Pharisee who, when a woman of dubious character anointed Jesus, could see only a sinner defiling him, and not an occasion celebrating human gratitude for divine forgiveness (Luke 7:39). It was all too possible to ignore or discount what is obviously good and to fail to see God's kingly power at work – like the scribes who could see only sorcery in a healing and healthful act (exorcism) such as God would delight to own (Mark 3:20–30). Wake up to the significance of what is happening in Jesus, in his message, and ministry! It was all too possible even for a John the Baptist to miss the significance of Jesus, because his message and life-style did not fit into John's assumptions and convictions (Matt. 11:1–6). It was all too possible for a Chorazin, or Bethsaida, or even Capernaum, despite all that they had seen and heard firsthand of Jesus' words and works, to prefer the comfort of a daily routine undisturbed by questions about primary values and ultimate responsibilities (Matt. 11:20–4).

There is *a disturbing quality about the urgency of Jesus' call*, a shaking of the foundations which those who want nothing but a quiet life are bound to resent and resist.

An Imminent Crisis

What was at stake was still more pressing. The single most frequently recurring theme in Jesus' parables is the warning of an impending crisis which required action NOW! Several of his parables are focused on an absent householder, for whose return servants have to wait, in hourly anticipation of his arrival (Mark 13:34–6; Luke 12:36–8; Matt. 24:45–51). In a similar vein he paints a vivid picture of a householder unprepared for the thief (Matt. 24:43). The parable of the ten virgins has the same message: The bridegroom is coming; make sure you are ready (Matt. 25:1–12, "The Kingdom of Heaven is like . . . "). So too the otherwise puzzling parable of the unjust steward: The day of reckoning is at hand, your guilt is about to be uncovered; act now before it is too late (Luke 16:1–8a). And the warning of Matt. 5:25–6: You are in the position of a guilty man about to be hauled into court; now is your last chance to settle with your creditor. Or the snatch of conversation in Luke 13:1–5, where reference is made to an incident where some Galileans had been killed by Pilate's soldiers, and to another where a tower had fallen, crushing several under it to death. Says Jesus, "Unless you repent you will all likewise perish." A disaster of much greater magnitude, but as sudden and as final as these more local incidents, is about to fall upon you.

In all this, it need hardly be said, Jesus took the prospect of divine judgment on human action and attitude with the utmost seriousness. He portrayed it as an imminent crisis which demanded immediate response. He made his hearers aware that any presupposition that life would simply carry on in its normal course was a dangerous and likely to be fatal delusion. The assumption that a pattern of life, which had been contrived over some time, could be maintained or simply adapted to new circumstances was fragile in the extreme and subject to the most devastating disproof. There is a human responsibility which dare not be ignored and which will be called to ultimate account sooner than one expects, and, if one downplays it, at a time when one is least prepared.

In Jesus' message this is tied into his expectation of the imminent coming of God's kingly rule in still fuller and final expression – within the lifetime of his own generation (Mark

9:1) – with all that that involved in terms of cosmic convulsion (Mark 13:24–30), and the coming of the Son of Man (Matt. 10:23). This creates difficulties for us today, since nearly 2,000 years have passed since Jesus so spoke. It raises important questions which go beyond the scope of this book, but which we cannot ignore and must at least mention, since they follow so immediately from the urgency which was a feature of Jesus' call to discipleship. To what extent, for example, can we interpret such language as a metaphorical way of heightening the urgency of a decision which is of final significance in shaping the course of a life? To what extent does it translate quite properly into warnings about the transience of all life and about the unexpected abruptness with which any life might end? Is our human physiology or character such that we actually need a sense of (chronologically) imminent judgment to jerk us out of our apathy, casualness, and self-absorption? Does the threat of nuclear holocaust, or of as yet unknown fatal viruses, fill the same role in twentieth-century perspective as an imminent, end-of-the-world expectation did in the first century? And not least, to what extent is it right to frighten people into a proper sense of responsibility and urgency?

These are large and difficult questions. And Christians ought not to duck them. But neither should such questions be allowed to obscure and diminish the challenge of Jesus at this point. That challenge can be summed up in simple terms. (1) The rule of God and its claim upon our lives is *too serious to be ignored.* It confronts us with issues of literally fundamental importance: Is God the ultimate reference point for human responsibility or not? (2) Response to the call of God's Kingdom is therefore vital: *the whole character of human life is literally at stake,* whether, in the final analysis, an individual's life will be determined by asking what God wants or only by consulting one's own selfish interests. (3) *The decision should not be de-*

layed; not just because life is short and some madman may release a fatal nerve gas without warning, but also because it might otherwise be too late to undo the damage a self-engrossed life has already caused, to the self and to others.

But what was the response for which Jesus called? How did discipleship of Jesus begin? Our text, at the head of the chapter, provides an answer in two words, "repent" and "believe."

"Repent . . . "

Convert

This is another word that causes problems in translation. As with kingdom, so with repent; we need to get behind the word which is so familiar to us. We need to ask what the word translated *repent* would have meant to Jesus' hearers. In Greek (the language in which the New Testament was written) the word had two predominant meanings. The primary meaning was "to change one's mind." And from that came the secondary meaning, "to regret, or feel remorse" – that is, over the view previously held. There is, of course, something of this in the stories Jesus tells to illustrate repentance. The "prodigal son" clearly feels remorse over his conduct in the "far country" (Luke 15:17–19). In the parable of the Pharisee and the tax collector, the latter is clearly portrayed as in some anguish as he prays, "God, be merciful to me a sinner" (Luke 18:13). And in Luke 17:4 we could very well translate the word in question: "If your brother says 'I am sorry,' you must forgive him."

But the word used by Jesus would have called for more than just a change of mind and an expression of regret. The more distinctively Jewish (as distinct from Greek) concept of repentance was much more radical. The nearest Hebrew equivalent had the meaning "turn round." As for example, in Isaiah's call for the wicked to forsake his way, and the unrighteous man his thoughts: "Let him return to the Lord, that he may have mercy upon him" (Isa. 55:7). Or in Jeremiah's repeated call to faithless Israel to "return" to God (Jer. 3:12, 14, 22). Or in Hosea's similar call, "Come, let us return to the Lord" (Hos. 6:1). In other words, in Hebrew thought repentance meant not simply feeling sorry, or changing one's mind. It involved a turning round, a radical alteration of the course and direction of one's life, its basic motivations, attitudes, objectives. This is why the best translation for the word used by Jesus would actually be "convert," understood in its literal sense, *"turn round," and head in a quite new direction.*

All this is important. Because it is very easy to cheapen the concept of repentance and diminish its demand. It can easily become a matter of mere *words.* This is why the sacrificial system was instituted – to show the seriousness of sin, that expressions of regret alone could not make wrong right; a death was necessary (Lev. 4–5). But such *actions* can just as easily become mere routine, a formal expression of regret which hardly penetrates to the heart and makes little or no impact on the rest of life. Hence the calls for circumcision of the *heart* (as in Deut. 10:16), and such denunciations as we find in Isa. 58. This was also John the Baptist's point in calling for a once-for-all baptism as the expression of repentance (Mark 1:4). It was too easy to think that relationship with God could be repeatedly injured and repeatedly restored by repeated washings. John called instead for a repentance which was so far reaching, so life transforming in its effect that it could be undertaken only as a once-for-all commitment. Otherwise it would mean less than nothing.

The call for repentance can also be undermined by being stereotyped in other ways. In particular, it would be a serious distortion to conclude that repentance is essentially a matter of feelings, and that there can be no true repentance without a conviction of guilt – as though the gospel is not rightly proclaimed unless it makes its hearers feel guilty. This is why it is not unimportant to notice that in our Gospels Jesus used the word repent/repentance itself on only a few occasions. In Mark, apart from Mark's own summary of Jesus' preaching, Jesus never calls for repentance as such. Matthew and Luke record a number of such utterances (particularly Matt. 11:21; 12:41; Luke 13:3, 5). But the Fourth Gospel avoids it altogether. And, we might add, Paul, the great missionary to the Gentiles, hardly used the word at all. In other words, we have only a handful of examples of Jesus calling for repentance in so many words.

A Radical Challenge

But this is where only to focus on the terminology itself can be very misleading. Such a focus on word occurrence or on repentance understood as conviction of sin can easily misrepresent what Jesus called for and the seriousness of what he called for. For, in the Gospels, Jesus' call for repentance is expressed much more frequently in *pictures* and *events* than in words. Consider, for example, parables like those already mentioned: the prodigal son (Luke 15:11–32), the Pharisee and the tax collector (Luke 18:10–14), or the empty house and the evil spirit(s) (Matt. 12:43–5). Or consider confrontations like those between Jesus and the rich young man (Mark 10:17–31) or Zacchaeus (Luke 19:1–9). And notice, not least, one saying of Jesus where he is recalled as using the more characteristic Jewish language as a variation: "Unless you *turn* and become like children, you will never enter the Kingdom of Heaven" (Matt. 18:3). So Mark's characterization of Jesus' preaching as a call to repentance (Mark 1:15) is not to be measured by word statistics alone.

More important, the parables Jesus used and the episodes in his ministry show just how serious and far reaching was the challenge he made and the response he called for. Jesus' call for repentance–conversion was something *radical*, as portrayed in the parable of the prodigal son, who quite literally turned round, wholly abandoning his former way of life (Luke 15:18–20). In the parable of the Pharisee and tax collector Jesus portrays it as *unconditional:* The Pharisee stated his claim upon God, and was not justified; the tax collector was justified precisely because his repentance made no conditions, attempted no justification, offered no excuses – "God, be merciful to me, a sinner" (Luke 18:13). The *comprehensiveness* of repentance–conversion is likewise indicated by such vivid little word pictures as Matt. 12:33 and 23:26: Repentance is a root and branch affair, a cleansing of inside and outside, affecting those who repent from the depths of their personality and right through the whole of their lives.

Not surprisingly Jesus saw clearly that the crunch would come for many on the matter of *material possessions* (as had John the Baptist, according to Luke 3:10–14). So it was in the case of the rich young man. For all the attractiveness of his character and the sincerity of his desire for eternal life, he could not face the transformation of life-style which would be involved in giving away his wealth and following Jesus.

Jesus looking upon him loved him, and said to him, "You lack one thing; go, sell what you have, and give to the poor, and you will have treasure in heaven; and come, follow me." At that saying his countenance fell, and he went away sorrowful; for he had great possessions. (Mark 10:21–2)

In contrast, Zacchaeus realized quickly what he must do. To respond to Jesus it was not enough simply to entertain Jesus in his home. "Behold, Lord, the half of my goods I give to the poor; and if I have defrauded any one of anything, I restore it fourfold" (Luke 19:8). It was in reference to such repentance that Jesus said, "Today salvation has come to this house" (Luke 19:9).

According to Luke, Jesus posed it as a more general challenge to his disciples: "Whoever of you does not renounce all that he has cannot be my disciple" (Luke 14:33). And, according to Mark, the disciples claimed indeed to have left everything to follow him (Mark 10:28). But the challenge was still more radical and more searching.

He who loves father or mother more than me is not worthy of me; and he who loves son or daughter more than me is not worthy of me. (Matt. 10:37)

Luke puts the saying in a still more severe form:

If any one comes to me and does not hate his own father and mother and wife and children and brothers and sisters, yes, and even his own life, he cannot be my disciple. (Luke 14:26)

The conversion called for by Jesus has to be that radical, that deeply reaching to and deeply transforming of even the most basic relationships. As Matthew's version shows, the talk of "hate" is simply a way of stressing the point, that the commitment Jesus calls for must transcend all others. It has to engage the whole person and transform wholly. Half measures are not enough.

Hence the saying which Matthew puts just before:

Do not think that I have come to bring peace on earth; I have not come to bring peace, but a sword. For I have come to set a man against his father, and a daughter against her mother, and a daughter-in-law against her mother-in-law; and a man's foes will be those of his own household. (Matt. 10:34–6; Luke 12:51–3)

Conflict of loyalty will be so inevitable for the disciple who turns completely around that Jesus can state it as one of his objectives in mission! Hence also the further saying whose importance is attested by the fact that all the first three Gospels have given it prominence:

Jesus said to his disciples, "If any one would come after me, let him deny himself and take up his cross and follow me. For whoever would save his life will lose it, and whoever loses his life for my sake will find it." (Matt. 16:24–5; Mark 8:34–5; Luke 9:23–4)

The discipleship Jesus calls for is *costly* because it asks, What are a person's true values and real welfare? and does not let anyone escape with half-answers and half-commitments. It is truly a matter of life and death.

Above all we need to reflect long and hard on Matt. 18:3: To convert is to become like a child. This strikes at the heart of all human evaluation of maturity and "grown-upness." For human society in general, childhood is a disadvantaged stage, something to be left behind. The ideal is adulthood, together, of course, with the independence, the power, the responsibility, the greater possibility for self-satisfaction which that stage of life brings. In contrast, to be a child is to be little, to be dependent, to need help, and to be receptive to it. What Jesus called for, of course, was not some kind of regression to infancy. He did not ask the would-be disciple to pretend to be a child or to act in a childish manner. His challenge was more profound: To realize that before God we *are* in fact little children, not able to live independent lives or to bear ultimate responsibility for ourselves by ourselves. As a matter of fact, adult "independence" is usually illusory and self-deluding; it hides an actual dependence on material possessions or on acceptance by family, friends, or peers. The repentance Jesus called for was a reversion to a more fundamental dependence on God as the source of our being, our meaning, our motivations. It was a call not for a surrender to irresponsibility, but for an affirmation of a responsibility before God, neither finally dependent on human "adult" values, nor undermined by the changing standards of human "adult" society.

In short, the repentance Jesus called for was not just a matter of saying "Sorry." It was not just a formal act of lip or hand which could leave heart and will unengaged and the rest of life unchanged. And it could not be reduced to feelings of guilt over particular sins. What Jesus called for was *conversion*, for a

turning round of heart and will and life, as well as a change of
mind. He called for a conversion which was the end of self-
serving and self-justification, a recognition of the delusiveness
of adult independence and material possessions, a realisation
of where a person's true worth and long-term good lies. He
called for a conversion to *God*, a yielding of life in and from its
innermost values and purpose to God's direction. Or, in a word,
what he called for was a submission to the rule of God before
all other claims on affection or commitment.

". . . and Believe"

Faith and Faithfulness

Mark 1:15 actually says, "Believe in the gospel." But the word
gospel is a Christian technical term, meaning "God's good
news to humankind." That is to say, it only began to be used in
this sense by the first Christians. All this means is that Mark,
in formulating his summary of Jesus' preaching, has expressed
it in terms which had become familiar in the early Christian
churches. Jesus himself almost always left the verb ("believe")
without an object, the implication being that the belief he
looked for was belief in God. It comes to the same thing, of
course. The gospel is "the gospel of God" (Mark 1:14). Here
specifically it is the good news of God's rule, the Kingdom of
God proclaimed by Jesus, the rule of God expressed in and
through Jesus' ministry.

As our text implies, the call to faith is the other side of the
coin from the call for repentance. Repent may be said to have a
more negative significance – turn away *from*. Whereas *believe*
has a more positive significance – turn *to*. And, as with repentance, what is envisaged here is not merely an intellectual act,
an assent to the truth of Jesus' statements (belief that); it has
much more the sense of "trust in," "rely upon." What Jesus

demanded of his hearers was not simply belief in his words, but trust in God.

Here again we need to inquire into the context of meaning which would have informed Jesus' hearers' understanding of what he asked of them. And once again it is an understanding that would certainly have been nurtured by what they had read and been taught in the Jewish scriptures. There we find that human faith has two basic aspects.

(1) It means *trust* in the trustworthiness of God, recognizing, as we might say, that God is God, and what that means in terms of assurance for those who rely upon God. The classic example was Abraham, as Paul and Hebrews knew well (Rom. 4; Heb. 11:8–12): Abraham who had been promised a child and who continued to trust God even when it appeared humanly impossible (Gen. 15:6); Abraham, who as Paul put it, "against hope, in hope believed" (Rom. 4:18); and Sarah, who as Hebrews put it, "by faith received power to conceive, even when she was past the age, since she considered him faithful who had promised" (Heb. 11:11). Another Old Testament (OT) writing which seems to have meant much to Jesus and which certainly was greatly cherished by the first Christians speaks of faith in similar terms. Second Isaiah, writing with the disasters of Judah's destruction and Jerusalem's desolation fresh in his mind, portrays the Lord, the God of Israel as no mere deity of a small, defeated, second-class nation, but as the one and only God, Lord of all. With all appearances wholly against him, he calls for this trust.

> "You are my witnesses," says the Lord,
>   "and my servant whom I have chosen,
> that you may know and believe me
>   and understand that I am.
> Before me no god was formed,
>   nor shall there be any after me." (Isa. 43:10)

This is the trust for which Jesus also called: trust that God is, trust that God's rule is what really matters and is dependable, despite everything and through everything.

(2) Faith also means *faithfulness*. In both Hebrew and Greek the same word covers both meanings. In Jewish thought Abraham was again a prime example of such faith–faithfulness, as expressed in his readiness to offer up Isaac, his only son of the promise. The Epistles to the Hebrews and to James reflect the same understanding (Heb. 11:17–18; James 2:21–2). In other words, faith came to expression in faithfulness, faithful obedience to God's will. Trust which did not manifest itself in action was a contradiction in terms. Paul too, even though he had a different axe to grind, was equally insistent that faith is not faith unless it is also faithful obedience (Rom. 1:5). So when Jesus called for faith we can be confident that he had in mind not simply assent to a form of words, or a passive expression of trust, but a reliance on God which would become the basis and motivating center for all conduct and relationships.

"Your Faith Has Made You Well"

The words repent–repentance were not particularly prominent in Jesus' vocabulary. But talk of *believing* and *faith* was a good deal more common: in Mark, thirteen occurrences, Matthew adds another eleven, and Luke, ten; in John, many times. What is most striking is that the majority of these references to faith (or lack of faith) occur in relation to miracles – nearly two-thirds of those in the first three Gospels (in Mark, eight out of the thirteen). To the synagogue ruler, Jairus, he says, "Do not fear, only believe" (Mark 5:36). To the father of the epileptic boy, "All things are possible to him who believes" (Mark 9:23). To the disciples in the storm on Lake Galilee, "Why are you afraid? Have you no faith?" (Mark 4:40). Here the call is for the same trust of which the Old Testament writers had spoken. What is called for is not a naive belief in miracles; nor, interestingly enough, faith in Jesus himself. The call is for trust *in God*, and in God's rule, in God's benevolence and care; for faith in Jesus as the channel through whom God's rule was coming to expression.

This was evidently what the Centurion recognized: that, like himself, Jesus was a man under authority, with power to bring about what he wished because he represented a higher power (Matt. 8:9). It was this insight, and the boldness to plead on its basis, which drew from Jesus the surprised comment, "Not even in Israel have I found such faith" (Matt. 8:10); similarly with the Syrophoenician woman in Matt. 15:28. Hence the phrase which occurs most often on Jesus' lips, "Your faith has saved you, made you well" – to the woman with the hemorrhage (Mark 5:34), to Bartimaeus (Mark 10:52), to the woman "who was a sinner" (Luke 7:50), and to the Samaritan leper (Luke 17:19). In each case what was in view was a trust in God's gracious rule, an openness to God's healing power through Jesus. Nor can it be characterized as a "sit back and wait for God to act in his own time" faith. This faith recognized that with Jesus, a window of opportunity had opened, a window of opportunity which might close again just as quickly (Mark 5:27–8). It recognized that in Jesus God's time had come (Matt. 8:8–9). It persisted, it argued with Jesus, it would not take "No" for an answer (Mark 10:47–8; Matt. 15:22–7). It was this faith, unyieldingly open to God's gracious outreach, which Jesus commended so strongly (Mark 11:22–4; Matt. 7:7–11).

Nor should the faith Jesus called for be characterized as faith just for a cure, trust only in a crisis. The healing, calming effect of such faith was only a particular expression of the daily faith of discipleship.

Why are you anxious about clothing? Consider the lilies of the field, how they grow; they neither toil nor spin; yet I tell you, even Solomon in all his glory was not arrayed like one of these. But if God so clothes the grass of the field, which today is alive and tomorrow is thrown into the oven, will he not much more clothe you, O men of little faith? Therefore do not be anxious, saying, "What shall we eat?" or "What shall we drink?" or "What shall we wear?" For . . . your heavenly Father knows that you need them all. But seek first his kingdom . . . and all these things shall be yours as well. (Matt. 6:28–33; similarly, 10:29–31)

Of course, Jesus is not inviting his disciples here to assume an attitude of irresponsibility, to act as though they were grass or lilies! His point is that the beauty and bounty of nature are a living, daily testimony that God is good, that God's rule is benevolent. His concern is to encourage his disciples to such a confidence in God, as a calm center in the busyness of daily life, as a tranquil basis from which the often weighty responsibilities of every day can be transacted, as a channel through which the same gracious power of God can be drawn, a resource to illumine intractible problems and to make unbearable burdens bearable. Here again what Jesus called for was faith as trust in God merging into the faithfulness of daily conduct and everyday relationships. When the center is thus secure, the radii hold the circumference firm. When priorities are right, the other things fall into place in their relative importance.

In short, what Jesus called for was not just belief, not just verbal assent to some credal formula, but trust, trust in God. What he sought to encourage in his disciples was an attitude, an orientation of life, a worldview or mind-set rooted in their innermost being, a base-rock conviction; and not an attitude or conviction which could be cherished inwardly or privately without making any discernible difference to the rest of life, but an attitude which informed and infused everything else, every other attitude and action, a fundamental conviction that motivated and gave character to the whole range of daily living and relationships. In other terms, he sought in his disciples an *openness to God* in the innermost center of their beings, an openness to God's will and God's time, an openness which could also be a channel of God's power shaping their lives in daily existence, healing and making whole. His call for faith was a call to make God's will central in motivation and action, and to let the rest fall in place, confident of God's fatherly provision for all that really matters. This is the wisdom of "babes," of those who have become as little children, a wisdom which is hidden from "the wise and understanding" of this world (Matt. 11:25).

Conclusion

Mark sums up Jesus' call to discipleship in these words, "The time is fulfilled, and the Kingdom of God is at hand; repent, and believe in the gospel" (Mark 1:15). In these words are encapsulated the challenge and the attraction which Jesus evidently exerted on so many of his contemporaries.

(1) Jesus' call to discipleship, then, is a call first and foremost *to recognize the reality of God's rule.* Jesus no doubt knew all too well that it is always easy to focus on the immediate and ignore the ultimate, to be absorbed by what is visible and forget the hidden realities of human existence, to concentrate on what lies within one's own power and forget that in the end one is but a pawn in the hands of forces far beyond one's control. The call to discipleship begins with a recognition of God, that God is the ultimate, the hidden reality behind all reality, the power beside which our power shrinks to infinitesimal insignificance.

(2) This call is a call to recognize that God's kingly rule is a

reality pressing upon those who hear Jesus' message, *summoning them urgently to decision*, a decision not to be delayed, an imminent crisis. The decision dare not be postponed, just because life is sweet, or business is booming, or other responsibilities leave no time. The crisis is closer than you think. The life so full, so busy, so meaningful, may soon be exposed in its shallowness and emptiness and meaninglessness.

(3) Such recognition inevitably requires *repentance* – a recognition not so much of guilt as of need, a confession not so much of sin as of immaturity, an acknowledgment of littleness before divine power, a reaffirmed dependence on resources beyond oneself and outside one's control. Such repentance is a response which goes beyond mere words or feelings or individual actions. Rather it is a response which turns the whole of life through 180 degrees and points that life in a new direction.

(4) Such recognition and response are the beginning of *faith* the medium of a relationship with God out of which one can live, a life lived in the light of God's coming kingdom, lived out of the resources of God's rule, with habits and responsibilities, conduct and relationships, needs and ambitions ordered by its priorities. So to believe is to seek first the Kingdom of God, and to rely on God to ensure that the other priorities and responsibilities fall into their proper place.

(5) In all this the disciple cannot forget that it is *Jesus* who brought this message, who issued the call to discipleship. Included here is the recognition that in him, in his message and actions, the kingly rule of God has already begun to come to expression. The urgency in part is because the character of God's kingly rule has so vividly and compellingly manifested itself in his life and ministry. Jesus' own teaching and life-style show what living in the light and in the power of the Kingdom should mean in the lives of those who repent and believe. This is why the call to discipleship in the final analysis is a call to follow *him*.

Chapter 3

Good News for the Poor

Blessed are you poor, for yours is the Kingdom of God. (Luke 6:20)

Introduction

Jesus' message was therefore both attractive and disconcerting: God's rule was active in his own ministry, in the healing of exorcism and the joy of the shared meal-table; but it was also pressing threateningly close, an imminent crisis which demanded urgent response. And the response he called for was both deeply challenging and reassuring: a repentance–conversion which was no half measure or easily dealt with in passing, but which required the concentration of a whole life in a life-determining decision; but also a faith which was a relaxing trust in and openness to the goodness and benevolent oversight of God.

To whom was this message addressed? To whom did Jesus primarily direct his ministry? Whom did he think would most benefit from or welcome this message of God's kingly rule? In calling to discipleship where did Jesus' priorities lie? Whom did he expect to make such a response? Two words sum the answer. We will focus attention on the first in this chapter and leave the second to the next.

The Poor

Jesus' Vocation

Jesus did not wait to be asked for whom was his message intended. He gave the answer without being asked. According to Luke he read the program and priorities for his mission straight out of the Old Testament – from the prophecy of Isaiah, in fact. He took the opportunity of being invited to read from the scriptures in his own home synagogue to announce his vocation.

He opened the book [of Isaiah] and found the place where it was written.

> "The Spirit of the Lord is upon me,
>> because he has anointed me to preach good news to the poor.
> He has sent me to proclaim release to the captives
>> and recovering of sight to the blind,
> to set at liberty those who are oppressed,
>> to proclaim the acceptable year of the Lord."

And he closed the book, and gave it back to the attendant, and sat down; and the eyes of all in the synagogue were fixed on him. And he began to say to them, "Today this scripture has been fulfilled in your hearing." (Luke 4:17–21)

In Isaiah the first task of the one anointed by the Spirit, and the primary purpose of this anointing, was that he should *preach the good news to the poor.* It was this anointing and this task which Jesus claimed for himself.

It should be said at once that there is some question about the strict historicity of Luke's account at this point. In the parallel accounts of Mark (and Matthew) nothing is said of such an announcement (Mark 6:1–6; Matt. 13:53–8), a strange omission of such a significant and revealing claim, had it been made by Jesus in that way on that occasion. And Luke's ac-

count appears very much like an elaboration of the much brief-
er account of Mark, filling out Mark's very bare statement that
Jesus "began to teach in the synagogue" (Mark 6:2). Moreover,
the way Luke's narrative develops, with Jesus referring
provocatively to the ministries of Elijah and Elisha *outside*
Israel and to *non*-Jews (Luke 4:25–7), strongly suggests that
Luke has presented Jesus' teaching in the synagogue at
Nazareth as already an apology for a mission beyond the
boundaries of Israel – an apology, indeed, for the mission to the
Gentiles which is the theme of Luke's second volume (Acts). In
short, it appears that Luke has done with this episode what
Mark did with his summary of Jesus' proclamation in Mark
1:15. He has set it at the very beginning of his account of Jesus'
ministry, the first episode to be narrated after Jesus' baptism
and temptations (like Mark 1:15). And presumably he intended
it to serve as a kind of contents page for what follows – a
program for Jesus' ministry, a summary (like Mark 1:15) of the
emphases which characterized Jesus' mission.

The significance of Luke 4:17–21 does not, however, depend
on the issue of its historicity or nonhistoricity. Luke probably
has done what storytellers and preachers have done down
through the centuries – fill out and elaborate a briefer narrative
to make its significance clearer. The more important question
is whether his elaboration is a fair representation of what Jesus
might well have said on that occasion, or a work of sheer imag-
ination. In this case the former is much the more likely, for the
simple reason that the same emphasis appears in at least two
other traditions of Jesus' teaching preserved in the first three
Gospels.

The first is contained in Jesus' reply to the question put by
John the Baptist from his prison cell (Matt. 11:1–6). The Baptist
was unsure whether Jesus was the one whose coming he had
predicted (Matt. 11:3). This was hardly surprising, since John
had depicted the coming one as a figure of fearful judgment

(Matt. 3:7–12). But Jesus' proclamation of the Kingdom seemed to be differently focused, more in terms of blessing than of judgment. And indeed, it is just this emphasis which Jesus brought to focus in his reply to John:

> Go and tell John what you hear and see:
>> the blind receive their sight and the lame walk,
>> lepers are cleansed and the deaf hear,
>> the dead are raised up,
>> and the poor have good news preached to them.
>> (Matt. 11:4–5)

Two points are of particular significance for us here: (1) As noted in Chapter 2, Jesus' reply evidently draws on three passages in Isaiah (29:18; 35:5–6; 61:1). But in each case the allusion is only to the blessings of the new age of which these passages speak. The warnings of judgment which they also contain (Isa. 29:20; 35:4; 61:2), and which the Baptist would have recognized, he passes over. But this is just what Luke portrays Jesus as doing in the synagogue at Nazareth, stopping his reading of Isa. 61:1–2 at the very point where Isaiah's message turns from promise to threat. (2) In the list of blessings in Matt. 11:5 the climax comes in the allusion to Isa. 61:1. By its position at the end of the six clauses, the proclamation of good news to the poor is where the chief stress lies. Somewhat surprisingly, it is not the dead being raised, but the fact that the poor are having the good news preached to them which Jesus presents as the chief feature and high point of his ministry. But this again is just what Luke portrays Jesus as doing in the synagogue in Nazareth – using Isa. 61:1 to state that his top priority was the announcement of God's good news to the poor.

The other tradition of Jesus' teaching which bears upon our topic is, of course, the text given at the head of the present chapter. In the sequence of Beatitudes the first blessing is declared on the poor, "Blessed are you poor, for yours is the Kingdom of God" (Luke 6:20). Matthew's version is slightly different (Matt. 5:3), and we will return to that below. The point to be noted here is that in both Luke's and Matthew's lists of Beatitudes it is the pronouncement of blessing on the poor which has first place. If, as many have suggested, the Beatitudes describe the characteristics of the people of God in the new age, then it is important to observe that the first characteristic of God's people in the new age is that they are the poor. Here again the implication is clear that Jesus has read his mission and its priorities in large measure at least from the prophecy of Isa. 61:1. One of his first tasks, if not the first task, is to proclaim good news to the poor.

We may conclude, then, that Luke's portrayal of Jesus' preaching in the synagogue at Nazareth was well rooted in the earliest memories of the first disciples, memories of Jesus' *own* priorities, as hinted at by allusion to Isa. 61:1, and as lived out in his own ministry. Indeed, it was probably as a result of Jesus' own use of Isa. 61:1, and the prominence he himself gave to its verb "preach good news," that the first disciples made the equivalent noun "gospel/good news" into a technical term for the message of Jesus and about Jesus (Acts 10:36; 1 Cor. 15:1; Mark 1:1). And for Jesus himself this good news was above all for the poor. Whoever else his mission was for, it was for the poor.

But who are "the poor"?

Who are the Poor?

Here again we need to consult the Jewish context of Jesus' teaching. For here once again Jesus was clearly drawing on a very strong strand of Old Testament teaching.

(a) In the Old Testament "the poor" are of course *the materially impoverished.* In the agricultural economies of the ancient Near East, ownership of land was the basis of economic security. Poverty might be the result of any one or more of a number of factors: bad harvests caused by natural disaster, enemy invasion and appropriation, indolence and bad management, malpractice by powerful neighbors, or entrapment in a cycle of debt at extortionate interest. The poor, then, were those who lacked a secure economic base. Like widows, orphans, and aliens, they were in an especially vulnerable position, without any means of self-protection.

In the examples cited in the next section the harsh reality of poverty is clearly illustrated: the day laborer who, owning no land of his own, must work for others, and who unless he is paid the same day will have no means of buying food and will go to bed hungry; the individual who has to pawn his one-and-only cloak and who needs to have it back before the day ends, otherwise he will have no means of warding off the cold of the night; those who have to depend on the generosity of the landowner for any share in the harvest. The social stigma of poverty is mirrored in a sequence of proverbs, which no doubt echoes the common wisdom of the time.

> The ransom of a man's life is his wealth,
>   but a poor man has no means of redemption. (Prov. 13:8)
>
> The poor is disliked even by his neighbour,
>   but the rich has many friends. (14:20)
>
> The poor use entreaties,
>   but the rich answer roughly. (18:23)
>
> Wealth brings many new friends,
>   but a poor man is deserted by his friend. (19:4)
>
> The drunkard and the glutton will come to poverty,
>   and drowsiness will clothe a man with rags. (23:21)
>
> He who tills his land will have plenty of bread,
>   but he who follows worthless pursuits will have plenty of poverty. (28:19)
>
> Remove far from me falsehood and lying:
>   gave me neither poverty nor riches; . . .
> lest I be poor, and steal,
>   and profane the name of my God. (30:8–9)

(b) In the prophets it becomes particularly clear that poverty is by no means always the result of individual fecklessness or slothfulness, of natural disaster or enemy action. It is also a social condition, with social causes, often the result of greed and manipulation on the part of others. Material poverty means also *economic and political powerlessness.* The poor are those who are vulnerable before other members of society who control economic and political power, and who are willing to use that power ruthlessly. Consequently, the poor are also the downtrodden and oppressed, those pushed by circumstances to the margin of society.

Two episodes during the monarchy well illustrate such power and its use. One is the story which Nathan the prophet tells to David to bring home to him his sin in taking Uriah's wife to be his own (2 Sam. 12:1–6). The story is of a rich man who had very many flocks and herds, and a poor man who had nothing but one little ewe lamb, which he loved like a daughter. But when a traveler visited the rich man, he was unwilling to have one of his own possessions killed to make a meal for the traveler, and instead took the poor man's lamb and prepared it for his guest. The degree of realism in the parable tells us much about the social reality of poverty and abuse of power possible in those days. The other is the account of Ahab's attempt to take over Naboth's vineyard (1 Kings 21). Even though Naboth had every right on his side to refuse to sell the land which was his birthright, King Ahab was able to have him executed on a trumped-up charge, with his property consequently forfeit to the Crown. Where such reasonably well-to-do people as Uriah and Naboth proved so powerless before the powerful, what hope had the poor?

(c) Since they are helpless and hopeless in the face of human oppression, the poor can rely on nobody except God. And so the idea of "the poor" comes to include those *who recognize their*

own weakness and look to God for help, since they can look
nowhere else.

> He saves the destitute from their greed,
>   and the needy from the grip of the strong;
> So the poor hope again . . .. (Job 5:16, New English Bible)

> For the needy shall not always be forgotten,
>   and the hope of the poor shall not perish for ever. (Ps. 9:18)

> Arise, Lord, set your hand to the task;
>   do not forget the poor, O God.
> Why, O God, has the wicked man rejected you
>   and said to himself that you do not care?
> You see that mischief and trouble are his companions,
>   you take the matter into your own hands.
> The poor victim commits himself to you;
>   fatherless, he finds in you his helper. (Ps. 10:12–14)

> This poor man cried, and the Lord heard him,
>   and saved him out of all his troubles. (Ps. 34:6)

The Jewish understanding of poverty as reflected in the Old
Testament, therefore, is neither simplified nor idealized. Start-
ing from the harsh, often brutal reality of poverty it recognizes
different dimensions of poverty – material, social, and spiritual. In all this we can speak quite properly of an Old Testament "theology of poverty."

A Theology of Poverty

The typical Old Testament response to poverty has three
strands, corresponding roughly to the three dimensions of poverty just outlined.

(a) Whatever the causes of poverty, the *fact* of poverty itself
lays *a responsibility on the nonpoor to provide for the poor,* a
responsibility not left to chance or goodwill, but safeguarded in
the law and custom that provided the basis of Israelite society.
This is most clearly spelled out in the book of Deuteronomy,

which itself provided the basic statement of Israel's understanding of itself as a people under God, chosen by God, and responsible to God. The extent of social provision for the weaker members of society is worth illustrating, even though it involves a lengthy quotation.

If there is among you a poor man, one of your brethren, in any of your towns within your land which the Lord your God gives you, you shall not harden your heart or shut your hand against your poor brother, but you shall open your hand to him, and lend him sufficient for his need, whatever it may be. Take heed lest there be a base thought in your heart, and you say, "The seventh year, the year of release is near," and your eye be hostile to your poor brother, and you give him nothing, and he cry to the Lord against you, and it be sin in you. You shall give to him freely, and your heart shall not be grudging when you give to him; because for this the Lord your God will bless you in your work and in all that you undertake. For the poor will never cease out of the land, therefore I command you, You shall open wide your hand to your brother, to the needy and to the poor, in the land. (Deut. 15:7–11)

When you make your neighbour a loan of any sort, you shall not go into his house to fetch his pledge. You shall stand outside, and the man to whom you make the loan shall bring the pledge out to you. And if he is a poor man, you shall not sleep in his [coat which he had given as a] pledge; when the sun goes down, you shall restore to him the pledge that he may sleep in his cloak and bless you; and it shall be righteousness to you before the Lord your God.

You shall not oppress a hired servant who is poor and needy, whether he is one of your brethren or one of the sojourners who are in your land within your towns; you shall give him his hire on the day he earns it, before the sun goes down (for he is poor, and sets his heart upon it); lest he cry against you to the Lord, and it be sin in you. (Deut. 24:10–15)

When you reap your harvest in your field, and have forgotten a sheaf in the field, you shall not go back to get it; it shall be for the sojourner, the fatherless, and the widow; that the Lord your God may bless you in all the work of your hands. When you beat your olive trees, you shall not go over the boughs again; it shall be for the sojourner, the fatherless, and the widow. When you gather the grapes of your vineyard, you shall not glean it afterward; it shall be for the sojourner, the fatherless, and the widow. You shall remember that you were a slave in the land of Egypt; therefore I command you to do this. (Deut. 24:19–22)

Such regulations make quite clear how the covenant between God and Israel was to be understood, and thus how life should be lived within the covenant. To be the people of God meant a life lived in a society regulated to make provision for weak and marginalized members of that society. It was not possible to be right with God without showing active concern for those who lacked the means of self-support. And this concern was not to be left simply to individual charity, but reinforced and maintained by legislation.

(b) The other side of the same active concern is the prophets' vigorous *condemnation of oppression of the poor*. The assertion of social responsibility for the poor was not regarded as an unreal idealization, or limited to a few. Wherever and by whomsoever it was ignored, the prophets spoke out in denunciation – whether the excuse was affairs of state, or of business, or of religion. The prophets were no respecters of persons. That is one of the main reasons why their words were remembered. A social and political critique was part and parcel of their religious message.

> Hear the prophecy of Isaiah:
> "The Lord enters into judgment
>   with the elders and princes of his people:
> 'It is you who have devoured the vineyard,
>   the spoil of the poor is in your houses.
> What do you mean by crushing my people,
>   by grinding the face of the poor?'
>   says the Lord God of hosts." (Isa. 3:14–15)

He denounces those who think they can be acceptable to God while ignoring their responsibility to others, those who say,

"Why have we fasted, and you see it not?
    Why have we humbled ourselves, and you take no
    knowledge of it?"
Behold, in the day of your fast you seek your own pleasure,
    and oppress all your workers. (Isa. 58:3)

Religious practice, however faithful and devout, if unaccompanied by active concern for the neighbor, is unacceptable to God.

Is not this the fast that I choose:
    to loose the bonds of wickedness,
    to undo the thongs of the yoke,
to let the oppressed go free,
    and to break every yoke?
Is it not to share your bread with the hungry,
    and bring the homeless poor into your house;
when you see the naked, to cover him,
    and not to hide yourself from your own flesh? (Isa. 58:6–7)

Equally outspoken is Amos:

Thus says the Lord:
"For three transgressions of Israel,
    and for four, I will not revoke the punishment;
because they sell the righteous for silver,
    and the needy for a pair of shoes –
they that trample the head of the poor into the dust of the
    earth,
    and turn aside the way of the afflicted." (Amos 2:6–7)
Hear this, you who trample upon the needy,
    and bring the poor of the land to an end,
saying, "When will the new moon be over,
    that we may sell grain?
And the sabbath,
    that we may offer wheat for sale,
that we may make the ephah small and the shekel great,
    and deal deceitfully with false balances,
that we may buy the poor for silver
    and the needy for a pair of sandals,
    and sell the refuse of the wheat?" (Amos 8:4–6)

The prophets recognized well that desire for wealth is almost bound to result in disregard for others, that acquisitiveness and exploitation go hand in hand. Such greed could even be accompanied by careful religious practice without any sense of inconsistency. Against all such the word of God spoke boldly and clearly.

(c) The third strand of the Old Testament theology of the poor is the affirmation of *God as the champion of the poor.* The reality of human society and acquisitiveness is such that the poor will always tend to be exploited; a society built on the competitive principle means that in order for there to be a winner, there must be a greater number of losers. In such a society, where law and custom do not provide sufficient protection for the poor, and where religion is still given a place of real honor, the final sanction is God, and the judgment of God. The character of God and the priorities of God are therefore of first importance. And in the Jewish scriptures there is no room for doubt: God is the God of the poor.

If the other strands of the Old Testament theology of poverty are more clearly expressed in the law and the prophets, this emphasis comes to clearest expression in the third strand of the Old Testament – for example, the psalmist.

> "Because the poor are despoiled, because the needy groan,
>   I will now arise," says the Lord:
> "I will place him in the safety for which he longs." (Ps. 12:5)
>
> You would confound the plans of the poor,
>   but the Lord is his refuge. (Ps. 14:6)
>
> Father of the fatherless and protector of widows
>   is God in his holy habitation. (Ps. 68:5)
>
> He raises the poor from the dust,
>   and lifts the needy from the ash heap. (Ps. 113:7)

There is, then, an impressive consistency running through the writings of the Old Testament on this subject, a consistency which warrants the description of an Old Testament theology of poverty. Fundamental to it is the insistence that ethics and spirituality cannot be separated, that individual, social, and religious responsibilities are inextricably interwoven; that the nation under God is a nation charged with responsibility to protect and provide for its weaker members; that exploitation, however dressed up and however much combined with religious profession, must be exposed and condemned without fear or favor; that those who call on the name of God call on one who considers the unprotected and vulnerable within society to be one of his main charges, and who expects a similar concern among his devotees.

It is this theology which Jesus would have been taught in his schooling and upbringing. It is this theology, no doubt, which informed his own thinking about the poor. It is this theology which he himself reaffirmed in his own teaching. No one should have been particularly surprised that Jesus shared this scriptural emphasis as a first priority of his own ministry. "Blessed are you poor, for yours is the Kingdom of God" (Luke 6:20).

But was his message then simply a restatement of old legal principle and prophetic protest? Or was there something distinctive in his teaching, here, too? How did his proclamation of the Kingdom bear upon his good news for the poor? Did the distinctiveness of his Kingdom theology add a further dimension to the Old Testament theology of poverty? And, not least, what did his reaffirmation of the Old Testament theology of poverty mean for his call to discipleship and for the character of the discipleship to which he called his hearers?

"The Kingdom of God is Yours"!

The familiarity of the first Beatitude obscures the surprising character of this assertion. Kingdoms do not usually belong to the poor, but rather to the wealthy and powerful. Of course, the use of paradox was typical of much of Jesus' teaching. But Jesus presumably was not simply endeavoring to attract attention. He had a message for the poor. This was part of the good news which he had been anointed by God to proclaim to the poor. But what did he mean? What did he want his hearers to take from these words? In what sense did the Kingdom of God belong to the poor? At that time there were several clear alternatives.

The Revolutionary Option – Take It!

One possibility was to bring in the Kingdom of God *by force*. The Kingdom belongs to the poor; therefore let them arise and claim their rights. After all, Israel was a conquered nation, under enemy occupation. And Roman taxation, on top of the tithes required by priest and temple, had simply proved too much for many small landowners struggling under an impossible burden of debt. Not a few had given up the unequal struggle and joined bandits operating from highland or wilderness lairs, as Jesus' hearers must have known well (cf. Luke 10:30). Jesus' words might encourage others to take the same way of violence and warfare. The poor could therefore see themselves as the vanguard of a new age more just than the golden age of David's kingdom when Israel was independent and triumphant over its enemies. And discipleship could be portrayed as the attempt to exercise God's rule by human will and effort, and thereby to bring in God's Kingdom by political and military means.

The theological justification for this option was straightforward: Israel was a theocracy; it therefore owed allegiance to no power other than God; consequently only God had rights of ownership and taxation. Nearly thirty years earlier Judas of Galilee had led a revolt in protest against the census of A.D. 6 (a census, of course, provided the information base for taxation). And some thirty years later the Zealots were to use the same theological argument to justify the most serious attempt to translate this option into reality, in the rebellion of A.D. 66. Some could well have been tempted to hear the first Beatitude in this sense. "The Kingdom of God is yours. You are the true heirs and proper executives of God's rule on earth. Act in confidence that God's royal authority is with you. Seize your inheritance by force."

In the modern period some have indeed argued that this is what Jesus actually wanted and advised. The supporting evidence is fragmentary and speculative and its chief elements can be summarized briefly.

(1)   Jesus was put to death as a messianic pretender – "King of the Jews" (Mark 15:26).

(2)   In Luke's account this is tied into the charge that he forbade the giving of tribute (paying of taxes) to Caesar (Luke 23:2).

(3)   A rather enigmatic saying of Jesus encourages his disciples to buy swords, and at least some resistance was offered when Jesus was arrested (Luke 22:35–38, 50).

(4)   The episode known as "the cleansing of the temple" may be a whitewashed record of an attempt to seize the temple (the temple being a potential stronghold of great military significance and strength, as well as being the major center of wealth in Palestine).

(5)   One of Jesus' closest followers was called a zealot – Simon (Luke 6:15).

None of this is very convincing. (1) Any decision by the high-priestly faction (who exercised power under the Romans) to have Jesus put away as an unwelcome messiah was bound to translate "Messiah" to the Governor, Pontius Pilate, as "King of the Jews," and as such a threat to Roman authority. (2) The "cleansing of the temple" reads more like an act of prophetic

symbolism; a larger, more concerted military operation would
certainly have met with immediate and stiff Roman opposition
from the Antonia fortress which abutted onto the temple area.
The argument that the tradition of Jesus' teaching has been
sanitized suffers from the old problem of assuming what it tries
to prove. (3) There is no evidence of "zealot" being used in the
sense of "guerilla, freedom fighter" as early as the period of
Jesus' ministry, whereas we know that it was used at that time
to denote someone "zealous" for the law (Acts 22:3; Gal. 1:14).
(4) John's Gospel also contains a tradition to the effect that
Jesus was offered the military option and deliberately refused it
(John 6:15). Moreover, he depicts Jesus as saying, "My kingship
is not of this world; if my kingship were of this world my
servants would fight . . . " (John 18:36). The words are probably
John's, but the spirit is that of Jesus. (5) And, by no means least,
the tradition of Jesus' teaching on forgiveness and love, preserved by Matthew, would have been impossible to combine
with any militaristic zealot sympathies or policy.

> You have heard that it was said,
>   "An eye for an eye and a tooth for a tooth."
> But I say to you,
>   Do not resist one who is evil.
> But if any one strikes you on the right cheek,
>   turn to him the other also; . . .
> and if any one forces you to go one mile,
>   go with him two miles. . . .
> You have heard that it was said,
>   "You shall love your neighbour and hate your enemy."
> But I say to you, Love your enemies
>   and pray for those who persecute you. (Matt. 5:38–44)

In short, we can be fairly confident that the revolutionary option was open to Jesus in one form or another. But it is also
sufficiently clear that Jesus did not commend or accept that
option. On the contrary, what he did commend, particularly a
love of neighbor which included love of enemy, must have been

highly unpopular with those who wanted to bring in God's Kingdom by force of arms. When Jesus said to the poor, "Yours is the Kingdom of God," whatever else he was doing, he was neither urging a peasants' revolt nor encouraging the poor to see their salvation as lying in their own power.

The Sectarian Option – Make It!

A second possibility was to disown the world and *withdraw* from it, to make a fresh start with a new model, a community where God's covenant was honored and the poor properly protected. In this case discipleship would mean withdrawal from the world, its failed ideals, its compromised social and religious structures, its entrenched vested interests. Like the first option, the second also started from an outright antithesis between the Kingdom of God and the present reality of human existence; and also from an outright rejection of any compromise with the status quo. But where the first option recoiled from the evil of an Israel ruled by any other than God, the second recoiled from the evil of a world ruled by Satan and his minions. And where the first tried to *change* the political reality of this world by violent means, the second *abandoned* this world as beyond redemption and waited for God to bring in his Kingdom in his own time.

That was the obvious practical expression of a theology most clearly expressed in Jewish apocalypticism, a theology and spirituality which thrived in Jewish circles for 100 to 200 years before and after Jesus. If this age is evil, perverted, and corrupted beyond redemption, then no time should be spent trying to redeem it. The only realistic alternative is to opt out of it, to cut yourself off from it so far as possible, to slough off its corrupting impurities, and to try to create a community which is a microcosm of life under God's rule in the age to come. The heavenly mysteries reveal the true nature of earthly reality (as under demonic influence). Properly understood, they also reveal the out-working of God's purpose for the elect few who have abandoned this world. And they may possibly even reveal the time scale for the fulfilment of God's final purpose. To seek to learn these mysteries, and thus to interpret the scriptures correctly, so as to provide guidance for life in this present evil world, and to prepare for the final intervention of God, was the chief task of the community which lived out of an apocalyptic perspective.

The most obvious exponent of this option at the time of Jesus was the community at Qumran, close to the northwest end of the Dead Sea. They believed not simply that the world was evil, but also that the rest of Israel had been deceived by the prince of darkness. In particular they were firmly of the view that the temple was corrupt, under a false priesthood, and observing the festivals at the wrong times (following a wrong calendar). Their solution is a classic example of sectarian response. They abandoned an Israel which, in their view, had abandoned the covenant with God. They went off to the wilderness, where they could expect to be closer to God (Moses and Elijah had been given their supreme revelations in the wilderness), a purified remnant. They formed themselves as a priestly community, whose quality of obedience to the law, as interpreted by their teacher ("the Teacher of Righteousness"), made up for the lack of sacrifice at the temple in Jerusalem. They did not seek to win others to their views, but welcomed any who came to join them. They saw themselves as the sons of light preparing themselves for the final battle against the sons of darkness.

Jesus would certainly have known about the community at Qumran. John the Baptist seems to have operated in the same stretch of wilderness, probably had some contact with it, and may have adapted his unusual practice of baptism from the ritual washings which were a prominent feature of the Qumran

group's communal life. We will also see later that Jesus probably alludes to Qumran's teaching and practice in at least one
part of his teaching. There is no hint, however, that Jesus commended anything equivalent to the option of withrawal exercised by the Qumran covenanters. On the contrary, for most of
his ministry he seems to have operated within the social and
religious structures of his society. According to the first three
Gospels he attended the Galilean synagogues regularly and
used them as a base for his teaching. In Jerusalem he likewise
frequented the temple, and in traditions retained only by Matthew, he is remembered as assuming the practice of temple
sacrifice (Matt. 5:23–4) and acknowledging the propriety of the
temple tax (Matt. 17:24–7). Not only so, but we have already
seen that Jesus' proclamation of the Kingdom did not result in
any attempt to cut himself off from the rest of society. The
point will be developed in the next chapter.

In short, when Jesus said to the poor, "the Kingdom of God is
yours," he certainly did not intend them to cherish it as a
heavenly mystery which they kept to themselves. He did not
see it as conferring on them a privileged status which required
them to separate themselves from the rest of society. He did
not imply that they should go off into the wilderness to found a
kingdom in miniature, preserved in its distinctiveness by its
distance from and condemnation of the rest of Israel. He did
not advocate the sectarian option for discipleship.

The Worldly Option – Live It!

This is one way to describe the option which Jesus seems to
have commended. "The Kingdom is yours," therefore live as
one who is under God's rule; whatever your circumstances,
live in the light and by the power of the coming Kingdom. Like
the other two, this option emphasizes that the Kingdom is
God's. Like the first, it recognizes the importance of human
action in the present with a view to the Kingdom; but not as a

means to bringing in the Kingdom, rather as a *celebration* of the kingly rule of God in the here and now. Like the second, it seeks to live a kingdom life in the present; but not at a distance from the world, rather *within* the world and with a view to making the world aware of God's rule. It rejects the revolutionary option, since it renounces the violence which would be necessary to overthrow the present world order in favor of an otherworldly order. It rejects the sectarian option, since it does not wash its hands of the world or abandon it for an otherworldly existence. It is a worldly option, since *it lives wholly within this world by otherworldly values and enablings.*

Jesus' own life-style can certainly be characterized in such terms. As we have already noted, he pointed John the Baptist to the marks of the new age which were already present in his healings and proclamation (Matt. 11:3–5). He saw his exorcisms, brought about by the power of God, as evidence of God's kingly rule happening in the here and now (Matt. 12:28).

> Blessed are your eyes, for they see,
>   and your ears, for they hear.
> Truly, I say to you, many prophets and righteous men
>   longed to see what you see, and did not see it,
>   and to hear what you hear, and did not hear it. (Matt. 13:16–17)

So too with the note of celebration so prominent in his ministry; because of God's reign, feasting was more appropriate than fasting (Mark 2:19), forgiveness could be enjoyed with directness and immediacy (Mark 2:5; Luke 7:48), salvation could be experienced and lived out of (Luke 19:8), and so on.

Since these emphases were so much part of Jesus' ministry, and so much bound up with his proclamation of the Kingdom, he could fully expect his hearers to understand the blessedness of the Kingdom in these terms. This is what the call to discipleship involved: *a call to live in the light of the coming Kingdom, just as Jesus himself did.* The poor should understand that this is what Jesus meant when he said "the Kingdom is yours"; that even in their circumstances there could be a living under God's rule, a living for God's reign, a celebration of God's Kingdom.

This last is easily said. But what did it mean in practice? Is there not still a danger of idealizing Jesus' message of good news for the poor? How did it work out in the reality of discipleship?

Good News

How is this message "good news for the poor"? If it neither offers the poor the chance to work out their frustrations in direct self-help action, nor the opportunity to escape from the harsh reality of their daily existence in an alternative society, is this "good news"? If it talks of celebration in a context of grinding poverty, is this not merely delusory, a dreamer's charter of no practical worth?

In fact Jesus' teaching on the subject, his worldly option, can best be understood simply as a wedding of the Old Testament theology of poverty with his Kingdom proclamation, a wedding wherein the theological perspective and severely practical ethic of lawgiver, prophet, and psalmist is given a heightened immediacy and urgency. It can be characterized in a number of ways.

The Power of Poverty

We have still to take account of the fact that Jesus' first Beatitude comes down to us in two forms – one from Luke, the other from Matthew.

Matt. 5:3:	Luke 6:20:
Blessed are the poor in spirit, for theirs is the Kingdom of Heaven.	Blessed are you poor, for yours is the Kingdom of God.

At first glance Matthew's version seems to be a much more spiritual message. There Jesus' blessing is not for the poor as such, but for the poor *in spirit*. That seems to say nothing at all about material poverty. It would be quite possible to envisage people who are well-to-do, *and* who have a humble spirit. Was Jesus then concerned more to inculcate an awareness of spiritual poverty than to encourage those living at or below subsistence level?

No! It would be quite wrong to set the two versions of the first Beatitude in antithesis; just as it would be equally wrong to conclude that Matthew's version denies the social implications of Luke's, or that Luke has twisted the spiritual message of Matthew's version. Both versions derive from and fully reflect the Old Testament theology of poverty. Both are legitimate ways of expressing the Hebrew understanding of "the poor." As we have seen, in the Old Testament the poor are the materially poor, those who lack possessions or a material base from which to defend themselves. As such they are also the oppressed; human nature being as it is, the improve off will usually try to improve their position by taking advantage of those weaker than them, and will usually succeed. As such the poor are also those who recognize their vulnerability and utter dependence on God, since God alone is their only and utterly consistent champion. The Hebrew understanding of poverty therefore is a spectrum, embracing both material poverty and confessed need of God. "The poor" and "the poor in spirit" are different ways of designating the same group of people.

Thus it begins to become evident that in both Jewish and Jesus' usage, "poor" is not only a negative term. It can also be a positive term. In using a word which had such a breadth of meaning, Jesus had in view an attitude as well as a fact: The attitude of those who recognize that reliance upon human strength and goodness (one's own or others) is an inadequate basis for life (or death); the attitude which recognizes that incividual and society need a source of strength and goodness beyond the merely human (God's kingly rule). To experience and live out of this recognition is the first rule of discipleship – good news for the poor. To live within this world, but by resources and values which are not dependent on this world, its ups or downs, that is a form of blessedness indeed.

The fact is that the materially poor are more likely to recognize the reality of their spiritual poverty than the materially well-to-do. That is why Jesus can state the Beatitude so starkly. The Kingdom belongs to the poor *alone*. God's blessings are only for beggars! They begin to be realized when poverty is recognized, the full extent of poverty. They begin to be experienced when we cease finding our life in what we own and control, and begin to live out of God's wealth of spirit and for God's Kingdom. God's blessing comes on the poor when they realize also that they are poor in spirit. *The power of poverty is the power to deliver from a delusive trust in wealth and prosperity*, the power to bring home the greater importance of treasure in heaven.

Hope for the Future

The good news for the poor is also one of *hope*; hope that in the day when God's kingly rule is fully realized, the injustices which they have suffered will be put right; hope that the values by which they have tried to live (poor in spirit) will finally be vindicated and provide the basis for the life of God's Kingdom; hope that the character and quality of Jesus' ministry and of the discipleship to which he called will prove to have been only the foretaste of something greater and more wonderful (the Kingdom of God). If the Kingdom which belongs to the blessedness of the poor is the Kingdom of Jesus' proclamation, it is a Kingdom not yet fully present, a Kingdom for whose coming they must pray.

The other side of the blessedness of the poor is the warning of judgment to come. Jesus' message of the Kingdom was also one of imminent crisis. There is a debt to be paid, one which must be paid now, since otherwise it will be too late (Matt. 5:25–6). The tree which does not produce good fruit will be cut down and thrown into the fire (Matt. 7:19). The foundations of the house are to be tested by flood and wind and rain, and if it is built on sand, it will fall to ruin (Matt. 7:26–7). Those who think they have found their life will lose it (Matt. 10:39). In the day of judgment it will be more tolerable for Tyre and Sidon, for Sodom and Gomorrah, than for those who have heard Jesus' clear message of good news and ignored it (Matt. 11:20–4). There is a danger that if you retain the hand or foot or eye which causes you to sin, in consequence your whole life will be thrown away as refuse (Matt. 18:8–9).

Of course, a doctrine of "final judgment" can seem to some a soft and easy answer to the plight of the poor – a cross between "pie in the sky when you die," and an unhealthy pandering to understandable human longings for revenge. And in modern secular society final judgment seems to be an outmoded idea, providing little if any of the constraint on human evil it once exerted. But perhaps even here the pendulum is beginning to swing back again. Certainly no other philosophy or ideology has been effective in stemming human acquisitiveness and injustice and oppression; quite the reverse, as human greed has become more global and sophisticated in its outreach and manipulation. All the more reason then, for the doctrine of final judgment to be "dusted off" and reexpressed in terms appropriate to today. All the more reason why Jesus' message, that God's final verdict will be in favor of the poor, should be reproclaimed as part of the good news for the poor today.

Hope for the future also means being able to be realistic about the present without despair. The hope of the poor is not disappointed by the continuing evidence of human greed and exploitation. For it never depended on an optimistic assessment of human character or on any suggestion that human society might evolve naturally into the Kingdom of God. *The hope of the poor is not hope in human effort or ideology, but in God.* Whatever permutations of social organization or structure emerge by evolution or revolution, the same forces of acquisitiveness and oppression will soon emerge and hold sway, and the same critique of the biblical theology of poverty will apply. The good news here is that to live as one of the poor before God is to live by resources and by values which will be shown to be right in that final day of reckoning.

Responsibility in the Present

The other side of the same coin is Jesus' repeated warning about the dangers of wealth.

> Do not lay up for yourselves treasures on earth,
>   where moth and rust consume
>   and where thieves break in and steal,
> but lay up for yourselves treasure in heaven,
>   where neither moth nor rust consumes
>   and where thieves do not break in and steal.
> For where your treasure is.
>   there will your heart be also. (Matt. 6:19–21)

Note again the combination of worldly practicality and spiritual (or psychological) insight.

> No one can serve two masters;
>   for either he will hate the one and love the other,
>   or he will be devoted to the one and despise the other.
> You cannot serve God and Mammon. (Matt. 6:24)

The story of the rich young man, who lived an exemplary life, but who loved his possessions too much (Mark 10:17–22) is an example of one who found the truth of this last saying. It is followed by a searching application.

Jesus looked around and said to his disciples, "How hard it will be for those who have riches to enter the Kingdom of God!" And the disciples were amazed at his words. But Jesus said to them again, "Children, how hard it is to enter the Kingdom of God! It is easier for a camel to go through the eye of a needle than for a rich man to enter the Kingdom of God." (Mark 10:23–5)

In a similar vein is the parable of the rich man who was being so successful that he thought he was secure for the future, and who said to his soul,

"Soul, you have ample goods laid up for many years; take your ease, eat, drink, and be merry." But God said to him, "Fool! This night your soul is required of you; and the things you have prepared, whose will they be?" So is he who lays up treasure for himself, and is not rich toward God (Luke 12:16–21).

Particularly sobering are the parables where condemnation is pronounced on the rich, not because they persecuted or despoiled the poor, but because they did nothing (Matt. 25:41–6; Luke 16:19–31). There were hungry people to be fed, poor people to be clothed and housed, prisoners to be visited, strangers to be welcomed, and they had done nothing – nothing to help them.

The danger of wealth is obviously that it encourages the attitude which is the reverse of that of "the poor" – self-reliance (or should we say wealth-reliance) and selfish ambition. The danger of wealth is that it becomes an instrument of power, and so corrupts, a means of influencing others and gratifying the self, a reason for adopting a rat-race attitude to life and for trampling others into the dust. The danger of wealth is that it encourages a disregard for spiritual values and resources, a trust in one's own strength and in what one controls. The power of poverty is that it discourages trust in one's own resources, facilitates a disengagement from the values of this world, and points to God as the measure of and means to lasting value. The poverty of wealth is that it makes it hard to distance one's true self from materialistic values, to disengage from attitudes which measure success by financial return, to recognize the character of the riches available to the human spirit. As material poverty so often goes hand in hand with an awareness of dependence on God (the poor), so material wealth too often goes hand in hand with pride and the selfish exercise of the worldly power which wealth usually brings.

Here too is an uncomfortable emphasis in Jesus' teaching too often ignored, and not least by members of today's rich First World. The good news for the poor is bad news for the rich! God's blessings are only for beggars! They are for those who, whatever their circumstances in life, know that before God they are only beggars! Although Jesus refused the option of political revolution, his message and life-style had revolutionary consequences, not least at this point, as we shall see more fully in the next chapter.

Childlike Freedom

There is one final aspect which ties back into what was said in the last chapter. The poor who seek the Kingdom of God, and who thus live responsibly toward others in the light of God's rule, are thereby *liberated* from the cancer of anxiety. It is not by accident that the words about laying up treasure in heaven and the impossibility of serving both God and Mammon (Matt. 6:19–21, 24) are followed immediately by the sublime advice not to take anxious thought about the bodily needs of daily life, and to consider the birds of the air and the lilies of the field (Matt. 6:25–34).

> Is not life more than food, and the body more than clothing? . . . And which of you by being anxious can add one cubit to his span of life or height? . . . Therefore do not be anxious . . . . (6:25, 27, 31)

Only those who recognize that value is not to be measured by the clothes one wears, that sustenance of the spirit is not ultimately dependent on food for the body, can be free from such anxiety. Only those who recognize that heavenly treasure has no correlation with treasure on earth, and that too much of the latter can be a positive disadvantage to gaining the former, are liberated from fear of failure in the competitive relationships of this world.

This is also a consequence of converting and becoming like children (Matt. 18:3). Of course, what Jesus calls for here is not any kind of childish or irresponsible attitude toward God. In contrast we need only recall his stern warnings against taking God's name lightly or making casual oaths (Matt. 5:33–7; 23:16–22), or his warnings about imminent crisis and final judgment, already examined. No, to become as a child is to recognize that our vaunted adult maturity is a form of self-deceit, that, as we noted in Chapter 2, before *God* we *are* little children. Here in fact Jesus' blessing on the poor meshes into his call to become as children. To become as a child is to recognize our poverty before God. The blessing of poverty is to live as a child before God, without our own means of support. In both cases, by means of his vigorous language and vivid imagery, Jesus calls his would-be disciples to recognize that our absorption with what we "possess" and control is a form of illusion; to recognize that much more important is our dependence on God for what we *are*. Only so will disciples experience the freedom of little children, wholly secure in their Father's love.

Conclusion

If we take this emphasis of Jesus' teaching and ministry with the seriousness it deserves, it points up some important features of the discipleship he called for.

(1) *Discipleship of Jesus begins with the poor*, with being poor, with recognizing one's own poverty. The first Beatitude, the text for this chapter, describes the first characteristic of

discipleship. Those who are not poor, who have not recognized their poverty before God, like those who cling to the illusion of their adult independence and control of their own destiny, have still to make a beginning on the pathway of discipleship. The Kingdom of God is for the poor. Only the poor enjoy its blessing. Only those who have given up trying to find their significance in what lies within their own power and have learned to live out of the resources of God's Spirit have discovered the blessing of God's rule.

(2) The fact that the idea of poverty thus envisaged includes at its heart a spiritual dimension (the poor in spirit) does not mean that it can be restricted to that interior dimension and spiritualized. The same word denotes also material poverty. The blessing Jesus pronounces is for the poor. When correlated with Jesus' words about the perils of wealth, as illustrated by the episode of the rich young man, it becomes evident that Jesus' discipleship is less likely to attract the rich. For it should be a discipleship of the poor, *characterized more by the fact and attitude of poverty* than by wealth and material concerns. At the same time we need to recall that some of those who followed Jesus did not find it necessary to give away all their possessions (e.g., Luke 8:3). In such cases the appropriate use of what wealth they had was part of their discipleship, and in this way, presumably, the attitude of poverty expressed itself.

(3) The out-working of the blessing on the poor in the life of discipleship did not take the form of a justification for violent revolution. But neither did Jesus envisage such discipleship in terms of a quietistic disowning of society and separation from the real world. *Social responsibility toward the poor and disadvantaged was part of the theology of poverty which Jesus reaffirmed in his own warnings against the perils of wealth.* If Jesus is right, the final judgment will not assume that all would-be disciples have had to choose between giving away all their possessions and following Jesus. But it will assume that

the nonpoor had a responsibility toward the poor. If Jesus is right, it will be the discarded and marginalized who are vindicated at the end, and the socially irresponsible well-to-do who are condemned. If Jesus is right, a discipleship of the nonpoor which lacks a sense of oneness with the poor, and so of shared responsibility for the poor, is in danger of forfeiting the blessing reserved for the poor, the blessing of the Kingdom.

Chapter 4

The Boundary Breaker

Those who are well have no need of a physician, but those who are sick: I came not to call the righteous, but sinners. (Mark 2:17)

Introduction

Even more notable than Jesus' concern for the poor was his concern for "sinners." According to Luke 4:18, Jesus claimed to be anointed by the Spirit "to preach good news to the poor." According to Mark 2:17 he claimed to have come with this specific purpose: to "call sinners." And it was this latter aspect of his mission which evidently drew the greater comment. His followers and companions are repeatedly called "sinners" by their critics in tones of manifest and deepest disapproval. He allowed "a woman of the city, a sinner" to touch him (Luke 7:37, 39). "Tax collectors and sinners" were attracted to him and he did not hesitate to receive them and eat with them (Luke 15:1–2). His readiness to dine with Zacchaeus drew the unfavorable comment that "He has gone in to be the guest of a man who is a sinner" (Luke 19:7). His eating a meal with Matthew/Levi and his friends occasioned the critical question, "Why does he eat with tax collectors and sinners?" (Mark 2:16). His whole life-style and style of ministry was deeply offensive to many: "Behold, a glutton and a drunkard, a friend of tax collectors and sinners" (Matt. 11:19). In the same vein Jesus himself did not hesitate to point out to his religious critics that "the tax collectors and the prostitutes go into the Kingdom of God before you" (Matt. 21:31).

For the Gospel traditions to have recalled so many such episodes and critical comments on this one subject means that his ministry to sinners must have been an important feature of his mission. If he came to preach good news to the poor, he came also to call sinners. If the blessing of the Kingdom is for the poor, the call to discipleship is for sinners. If then the would-be disciple must become as a child, if the first characteristic of discipleship is the acknowledgment and attitude of poverty, what is this further aspect of the discipleship to which Jesus called? What did Jesus mean when he said he had come "to call sinners"? Why sinners?

Who Are the Sinners?

It would be all too easy to assume that the meaning of "sinner" is obvious. A sinner is one who has offended against God. All are sinners, as Paul long ago pointed out (Rom. 3:23). Therefore Jesus came to call everyone without exception. And thus might one fall into a familiar evangelistic routine and theological rationale. But, as always, there is a danger of imposing meaning upon the ancient text, of hearing its words with the meanings which have become familiar to us by long personal or traditional usage. Here once again, then, it is necessary to hold our own understanding of the key word in suspense until we have checked whether the ancient usage accords with the one more familiar to us. And here again it is necessary to ask what Jesus and his critics would have understood by the word, to investigate the context of language and idiom within which the word had its meaning for both Jesus and his critics. *They* had a clear idea of who or what a "sinner" was. And only if we understand the connotation they gave to the word will we be in a position to appreciate the force of the criticism made of Jesus. Only if we know *who* the sinners were, and *why* they were so designated, will we be able to grasp the significance of his coming "to call sinners."

Lawbreaker

In Jewish thought the most straightforward definition of sinner is "one who breaks or disregards the law." This is evident particularly in the Psalms, where in the Greek rendering of the Psalms the word often used means literally "lawless." In English versions the word "sinner" is regularly synonymous with or equivalent to "wicked." For example:

> Blessed is the man
>   who walks not in the counsel of the wicked,
> nor stands in the way of sinners,
>   nor sits in the seat of scoffers;
> but his delight is in the law of the Lord,
>   and on his law he meditates day and night. (Ps. 1:1–2)

> Take me not off with the wicked,
>   with those who are workers of evil,
> who speak peace with their neighbours,
>   while mischief is in their hearts. (Ps. 28:3).

> I am distraught by the noise of the enemy,
>   because of the oppression of the wicked.
> For they bring trouble upon me,
>   and in anger they cherish enmity against me. (Ps. 55:2–3)

> Let sinners be consumed from the earth,
>   and let the wicked be no more! (Ps. 104:35)

> Hot indignation seizes me because of the wicked,
>   who forsake your law. (Ps. 119:53)

> Salvation is far from the wicked,
>   for they do not seek your statutes. (Ps. 119:155)

From this small sample it is clear that (1) the sinner is a wicked person, a "worker of evil"; and (2) sin is defined in relation to the law, as failure to observe the law, as forsaking the law. The sinner stands in sharp contrast to one who loves the law, a lawbreaker in contrast to the lawkeeper.

The law therefore is at the heart of the Jewish concept of sin and the sinner. And this is not to be understood simply in terms of individual morality. The law also defined the people. It had been given by God as part of God's covenant with Israel. It defined their response to God. It told them how to live as the people of God. God had chosen Israel to be God's people, had delivered them from slavery in Egypt. The law given at Sinai was their part of the bargain, their response to God's electing and liberating grace. This conviction is deeply enshrined in the central statements regarding the law in the Old Testament. For example, the Ten Commandments began with the words:

> I am the Lord your God,
>> who brought you out of the land of Egypt,
>> out of the house of bondage; (Exod. 20:2)

and then follows the list of the ten "You shall," "You shall not" commands. The Book of Deuteronomy, the classic statement of Israel's covenant theology, is structured in just the same way. "God delivered you from Egypt, therefore . . .." "Remember you once were slaves and how God dealt with you; therefore . . .." "Since God has given you the land as your inheritance, therefore . . .." On this understanding sin is not simply individual disobedience, but disregard for the covenant, action inappropriate to the people of God. Sin is *a social act*, with social consequences, as was soon illustrated in the episode of Achan (Josh. 7).

A point needs to be underlined here, since it has often been misunderstood in Christian tradition. This basic Jewish understanding of sin and law was not a form of legalism. The law did not come before the covenant. At no point was it stated that God made his covenant with Israel because Israel kept the law.

Keeping the law was *not* understood as a means of earning the right to be God's people. On the contrary, in Jewish thought the law was given *with* the covenant. Keeping the law was what being the people of the covenant meant. Faithfulness to the law marked out the people of God precisely as the people of the law. In short, keeping the law was not a means of getting *into* the covenant, but the way of living *within* the covenant.

Gentile and Apostate

In Jewish understanding, therefore, the law marked out the people of God. The covenant people was coterminous with those who had been given the law and who lived within the law. In other words, the law defined the boundaries of the people of God. And thus the concepts of sin and sinner gain a further dimension. For, since sin means breach of the law, the sinner by definition is one who is *outside the law*, which is to say, outside the people of God, outside the boundary marked by the law, outside the people who by definition are those who live within the law.

In the first place that meant *Gentiles*. The Gentile, that is, the non-Jew, is by definition outside the covenant people, that is, "outside the law, without God." This attitude is reflected most clearly in several of the Pauline letters. In Rom. 2:12–14, Gentiles are defined precisely as those "without the law," in contrast to those "under the law" – "Gentiles, who do not have the law." Similarly, in 1 Cor. 9:20–1, Jews are defined as "those under the law," in contrast to "those outside the law" (i.e., Gentiles). And in Eph. 2:12, Gentiles are described as "alienated from the commonwealth of Israel, and strangers to the covenants of promise, having no hope and without God in the world."

Consequently it was natural to equate "Gentile" with "sinner." Since the sinner was by definition "outside the law," an outlaw, the Gentile was by definition a sinner.

> The wicked shall depart to Sheol,
>   all the nations (Gentiles) that forget God. (Ps. 9:17)
> We who are Jews by birth and not Gentile sinners . . . (Gal. 2:15)

The same equation is reflected even in the tradition of Jesus' words – Jesus speaking from a Jewish perspective. In the garden of Gethsemane Jesus says, "The Son of man is betrayed into the hands of sinners" (Mark 14:41), where the betrayal is understood as a "handing over" (same word) to the Roman (Gentile) authority for execution (Mark 15:1, 10, 15). And in the different versions of the same teaching in Matthew and Luke the same equation is implicit: "Do not even the Gentiles do the same?" (Matt. 5:47); "For even sinners do the same" (Luke 6:33).

The plot thickens, however, when we see how the same logic worked out in relation to *apostates*. What of those Jews who break the law? The law itself provided atonement by sacrifice for less serious breaches of the law. But what of those members of the covenant people who by their actions in effect disown their covenant status? What of Israelites who fail to keep their part of the covenant, who do not live in accordance with the law, within the law, but who live in disregard for the law, outside the law? They too are sinners. By their actions they have put themselves outside the boundaries of lawful conduct, outside the boundaries of the covenant people. This use, of *sinner = apostate*, became established in the period of the Maccabean crisis. The crisis was provoked precisely because many Jews began to live like Greeks; they ignored the law which marked out the distinctive features of the covenant people. In the eyes of the Maccabean loyalists they were apostates, sinners (1 Macc. 7:5; 9:23, 58, 69; 11:25). The same is true of the popular attitude at the time of Jesus toward tax collectors. By their collaboration with the Roman occupation, tax collectors had put themselves outside the boundaries of conduct appropriate to the people of God; hence the natural association, "tax collectors and sinners," and the equation and association in Matt. 5:46–7 and Luke 6:32–4 – tax collectors, sinners, Gentiles.

Righteous and Sinner

The Maccabean crisis firmly established the idea that sinners were not merely Gentiles but also *Jews who had abandoned the covenant*. Loyalty to the nation became defined as loyalty to the law; naturally so, since the nation was defined as the covenant people of God precisely by the law given it by God. Particular laws became test cases, especially circumcision and food laws. Inevitably so, since these laws more than any other marked out the distinctiveness of Jews from other peoples; and since, for the same reason, the Syrian overlords focused on them in their attempt to obliterate the distinctiveness of Judaism.

According to the decree, they [the Syrians] put to death the women who had their children circumcised, and their families and those who circumcised them; and they hung the infants from their mothers' necks. But many in Israel stood firm and were resolved in their hearts not to eat unclean food. They chose to die rather than be defiled by food or to profane the holy covenant; and they did die. (1 Mac. 1:60–3)

With the disintegration of the Syrian Empire through the latter decades of the second century B.C. the Maccabees were able to sustain and establish their position, and the view of Israel's covenant status and obligation enshrined in the Maccabean writings became the dominant self-understanding of loyal Jews. But in the aftermath of the Maccabean crisis the covenantal heritage became disputed and contested. Different groups emerged within Israel, each laying claim to be the true defend-

ers and observers of the covenant, each denouncing other Jews
for their failure to observe the law adequately.

The best-known examples are the Pharisees and the Essenes.
The title "Pharisees" itself is probably a nickname, meaning
"separated ones." That is to say, they separated themselves
from other Jews by their conduct and life-style in order to
observe the law as they thought it should be observed. From
the early rabbinic traditions we can see that they wanted to
treat the whole land as sacred, as sharing in the holiness of the
temple, where God had put his name. Consequently they tried
to live at the level of holiness and purity required of priests in
the temple. As we shall see shortly, this concern came to particular focus in their observance of the food laws and in their
desire to maintain the purity of the meal table. The Essenes
took the same logic even further. The community at Qumran
had separated themselves more radically from the rest of Israel
by retreating to the wilderness. There they made a special
point of insisting on observance of the law as they understood
it. In their eyes, only they were being faithful to the covenant,
only they were keeping the law. In each case the zeal and dedi-
cation were impressive, and each was highly admirable in its
own way.

The consequence, however, was that such groups regarded
those *outside their group* as effectively apostates. To disagree
with their understanding and practice of the law was to disregard the law. To be outside the group was to be outside the
boundary marked by the law, to be "sinners." The Jewish writings of this period for the most part represent the views of these
groups (e.g., 1 Enoch, Jubilees, Psalms of Solomon, the Community Rule from Qumran). In them the older contrast between the righteous and sinners is given a sectarian twist. The
righteous are not simply Israelites or Jews, not simply those
who "keep the law." The righteous are *the members of the sect*,
those who keep the law *as understood by the group*. And "sin-

ners" are not just Gentiles, or those who break the law in ways
that any Jew would recognize. They are Jews who disagree with
the group's sectarian interpretation of the law; sinners, not in
some absolute sense, but in the judgment of those who thought
that their understanding of righteousness was the only correct
one. Those who were unacceptable to them, "sinners," they
naturally assumed were unacceptable to God.

Here we can see an attitude which history shows to be characteristic of fundamentalist groups, of whatever religion. These
groups within Judaism at the time of Jesus indeed provide classic demonstration of typical features of fundamentalism.

(1)   A specific and tightly defined interpretation of a faith
      and heritage more widely claimed and practised by
      others.
(2)   A fierce insistence that their understanding and prac-
      tice is the only correct one, the only one acceptable
      to God.
(3)   A denunciation of all variant and alternative in-
      terpretations and forms; the closer the variation, the
      more strident the denunciation. Thus the sectarian
      righteous have always found it necessary to disown
      fellow religionists as sinners.

The Boundary Breaker

Sinners not Righteous

It is against this background that the language of our text has to
be understood, "I came not to call the righteous, but sinners"
(Mark 2:17). Jesus here was responding to a criticism leveled
against him by one or more of the groups (sects) operating at
that time within Judaism. They saw themselves as the righteous, and condemned others as sinners. They criticized Jesus

because he consorted with people, Jews, who were outside their group. He ate with people, Jews, who made light of the points of law which they regarded as fundamental expressions of covenant obedience, test cases of covenant loyalty. Jesus, as prophet and teacher, ought to have approved a high standard of law observance. Instead, he made himself one with sinners.

Not only so, but Jesus accepted the criticism and turned it into a statement of positive intent. The righteous, so concerned with their own standing before God, so intent on maintaining it without blemish, did not need to hear the message of salvation. Those who devote so much of their energies to keeping healthy do not need a doctor (Mark 2:17). To the elder son in the parable of the prodigal son, the father says reassuringly, "Son, you are always with me, and all that is mine is yours" (Luke 15:31). Jesus does not fall into the trap of reversing the categories, of assuming that it is the righteous who by definition are *un*acceptable to God. Elsewhere he does warn that to make such righteousness a claim upon God *is* likely to prove unacceptable to God (Luke 18:14). But here it is his mission to those categorized by the righteous as sinners on which Jesus focuses attention. *He came to call precisely those whom the most religious of his fellow Jews rejected as having put themselves outside the scope of God's covenant provision.*

Whether the jibe "sinners" was leveled at every Jew outside the group involved, or was specifically directed against only a few who set themselves in blatant disregard for the distinctive claims of the group, we cannot tell. On the other hand we cannot assume that "sinner" was used only for criminals and delinquents, those generally recognized by all Jews as "wicked" and "lawless." The fact that "sinner" is set here in antithesis to "righteous" is clear indication that we are dealing with sectarian categories. Sinners are those of whose conduct the righteous disapprove. What the group regarded as unacceptable to them, they thought was unacceptable to God; they regarded it as unacceptable to them because they thought it unacceptable to God, a breach of the terms of the law of the covenant.

It was this claim which Jesus disputed, this specifying in detail of what (it is assumed) God approves and disapproves of, this drawing of boundaries which determine who is in and which shut others out. The Gospels indicate at least three areas where Jesus showed himself at odds with such sectarianism. Each focuses on an issue which the righteous would have seen as a test case of covenant loyalty. In each case Jesus' mission to sinners cut across current conventions and left him exposed to the critical fire of those who saw themselves as the defenders of orthodox covenant practice.

Table-Fellowship

Jesus' practice of eating in company was clearly a regular and important feature of his ministry. He is remembered as accepting many invitations to dine – with Pharisee, as well as friend, as well as tax collector (particularly by Luke – 5:29; 7:36; 10:38; 11:37; 14:1). His action as host, in blessing the bread and breaking it, is recalled as a familiar act (Luke 9:16; 24:30–1, 35). We have already noted that he used the metaphor of the banquet to depict the blessings of God's Kingdom, and practiced his table-fellowship as an anticipation of that banquet (particularly Luke 14:1–24). And it is already sufficiently clear that this practice of table-fellowship was a focus of many of the complaints brought against him.

The Son of man came eating and drinking, and they say, "Behold, a glutton and a drunkard, a friend of tax collectors and sinners!" (Matt. 11:19)

The scribes of the Pharisees when they saw that he was eating with tax collectors and sinners, said to his disciples, "Why does he eat with tax collectors and sinners?" (Mark 2:16)

The reasons why the meal table proved such a contentious issue would have been obvious to Jesus and his audiences.

(1) In the Middle East the meal table had a quasi-sacred character. It was a religious act: It expressed religious obligations and was reinforced by religious sanctions. This made the sharing of a meal, the act of hospitality, something sacred in turn. It was, and still is today, a mark of acceptance and friendship. When the host blesses the bread and breaks it, he distributes it to those with him at the table, so that they may share in the blessing spoken over the bread. Naturally, then, members of a sect would wish to restrict the scope of their table-fellowship. They could not offer the acceptance of the table to those whom they regarded as unacceptable, as sinners.

(2) In the Maccabean period and thereafter food laws and ritual purity had become test cases of covenant loyalty. In the Maccabean crisis itself, as we have already seen, maintenance of the food laws had resulted in martyrdom (1 Macc. 1:62–3); and martyrdom always gives a deeply emotive edge to the cause in question. Anyone who ignored the food laws would be likely to bring upon himself the charge of trampling underfoot the blood of the martyrs. This conviction was reinforced in the popular stories of the day – Daniel, Judith, Tobit, to name but the three best known. In each case the hero or heroine was notable for devoted observance of the food laws (Dan. 1:8–16; Tobit 1:10–12; Judith 12:1–4, 19). In each case it was their loyalty to the covenant, as expressed in their devoted observance of the food laws in adverse conditions, which God signally honored. So when Peter on the rooftop in Joppa saw a vision of a sheet let down from heaven containing all sorts of animals, and heard a voice inviting him to "Rise, kill, and eat," his response was predictably Jewish: "No, Lord; for I have never eaten anything common or unclean; nothing common or unclean has ever entered my mouth" (Acts 10:10–14; 11:5–8).

This was not a particularly sectarian attitude, just the attitude of a devout Jew who took the practice of his religion seriously. With how much greater horror would one of the "righteous" have contemplated a meal table where the food laws were not scrupulously observed.

We also know that, at the time of Jesus, the Pharisees and Essenes in particular regarded the meal table as a matter of peculiar sensitivity. For some at least of the *Pharisees* the meal table was precisely the point at which their attempt to maintain the purity of the temple in their daily life was most at risk. It was not simply a matter of abstaining from the flesh of unclean animals, or of ensuring that the animal had been properly killed and the blood drained off (kosher meat). Most observant Jews of the time would certainly have been careful in such matters. It was more the problem of whether food bought in the marketplace had been properly tithed; whether the food and the dishes and utensils used in preparing it had been maintained with adequate purity; whether someone with some sort of discharge had been sitting or lying on the couch at the meal table. A sinner by definition was one who did not maintain that level of purity, who was careless about such things, who perhaps disputed in word or deed the necessity of such scrupulous purity.

Similarly with the *Essenes.* As with Jesus, the communal meal was an important part of the common life at Qumran. As with Jesus, the communal meal already anticipated and reflected the character of the messianic banquet in the age to come. But for the covenanters at Qumran this meant preserving the common meal for the members of the community alone. The purity of the meal should not be infringed by any outsider. According to the rule of the community, even the novice was not to be admitted to the common meal until he had completed his novitiate (one or two years). Only when he had demonstrated his understanding and observance of the law (as interpreted in the community) could he take his place at the community meal (1QS = Community Rule 6). A Jesus who welcomed sinners to his table and ate with them would be regarded as beyond the pale by the Qumran group, however much he spoke of the Kingdom of God.

Jesus in turn was sharply critical of those who attacked his practice of table-fellowship. There is no suggestion in our sources that Jesus was criticized by the Essenes, though there is more than a hint in Luke 14:13 and 21 that Jesus expressed strong disapproval of Qumran teaching at this point. To this question we will return in Chapter 5. The main attacks on Jesus' table-fellowship recorded in the Gospels, however, are usually attributed to Pharisees. And there is clear testimony that Jesus did not hesitate to respond in blunt terms to such attacks.

In particular, Mark 7:1–23 contains a forthright rebuke of false priorities. The Pharisees' concern for ritual purity at the meal table was characteristically expressed in purification of the hands. The hands were most susceptible to impurity since in the marketplace they might well touch, even inadvertently, people or things that were in a state of impurity. And hands would need to be washed between courses lest they resulted in an inadmissible mixture of different foods. In Jesus' view such scrupulosity gave these already traditional interpretations of the law greater importance than the law itself (Mark 7:8). More seriously, this overwhelming concern with impurity caused by external sources gave it a false importance and obscured and diminished the importance of inward purity (Mark 7:14–23). Here Jesus cuts to the heart of the sectarian classification into the righteous and the sinner. For, if purity and righteousness are not visible, are not determined by outward actions, are not testable in terms of standards to be observed, then it becomes impossible to draw such a clear dividing line between what is acceptable and what unacceptable, between the righteous and the sinner.

So Jesus' practice of table-fellowship was not only an expression of the good news of God's kingly rule. It was also an implicit critique of a Pharisaic definition of acceptability, of a Pharisaic practice which classified many fellow Jews as sinners, effectively outside the law and the covenant, like the Gentiles "without God in the world." *What to many Pharisees was a sinful disregard for covenant ideals was for Jesus an expression of the gospel itself.* People they regarded as unacceptable, Jesus proclaimed by word and act to be the very ones whom God invited to his royal banquet. In the parable of the Pharisee and the tax collector it is clear that he rejects the "us and them" attitude which such Pharisaic piety fostered.

The Pharisee stood and prayed thus with himself, "God, I thank thee that I am not like other men, extortioners, unjust, adulterers, or even like this tax collector. I fast twice a week, I give tithes of all that I get." (Luke 18:11–12)

In pointed contrast, the tax collector stands "far off" and beats his breast saying, "God, be merciful to me a sinner!" And, says Jesus, it is the latter who was accepted by God, not the former (Luke 18:13–14). Not assertion of acceptability, but confession of unacceptability is what is owned by God. In striking antithesis to such Pharisaic boundary drawing, Jesus showed himself *more critical of those who condemned sinners than of the sinners themselves.*

Sabbath

Observance of the seventh day as a day of sabbath rest also provided an important distinguishing mark of the good Jew.

And the Lord said to Moses, "Say to the people of Israel, You shall keep my sabbaths, for this is a sign between me and you throughout your generations, that you may know that I, the Lord, sanctify you. You shall keep the sabbath, because it is holy for you; every one who profanes it shall be put to death; whoever does any work on it, that soul shall be cut off from among his people. . . . Therefore the people of Israel shall keep the sabbath, observing the sabbath throughout their generations, as a perpetual covenant. It is a sign for ever between me and the people of Israel that in six days the Lord made heaven and earth, and on the seventh day he rested, and was refreshed. (Exod. 31:12–17)

With such a clear statement there could be no doubt. Observance of the sabbath was a fundamental part of God's covenant with Israel, a mark of Israel's set-apartness as the people specially chosen by God to be God's own. Breach of it was a breach of the covenant itself; to ignore the sabbath law and work on the sabbath warranted nothing less than complete exclusion from the people of the covenant.

Similarly in Isaiah 56:1–7, observance of the sabbath is a critical factor in showing the acceptability of those who would otherwise be unacceptable – the Gentile (outside the law) and the eunuch (physically maimed). Here again sabbath and covenant go together: To "keep the sabbath" is to "hold fast to the covenant" (56:4, 6). If, according to the law, nonobservance of the sabbath is sufficient to exclude an Israelite from the covenant people, according to the prophet, observance of the sabbath will be sufficient to include the outsider within the benefits of the covenant. The eunuch who keeps the sabbath will be given a place of honor within God's house; the foreigner who keeps the sabbath will find his prayers and offerings in the temple accepted by God (56:4–5, 6–7). Once again the importance of the sabbath to Jewish self-understanding is underlined. Once again the sabbath has a crucial boundary-marking function, dividing those who are in from those who are out.

In the century prior to Jesus we see the same scrupulosity which had set such tight boundaries round the meal table transforming the sabbath law. The same concern to draw the definitions of acceptable behavior more clearly resulted in increasingly more-detailed rulings about the sabbath, as is evident already in the book of Jubilees, probably written more than 100 years before Jesus' birth. In Chapter 2 the older statements are reinforced, but the simpler law against working on the sabbath is already beginning to be elaborated.

And so you must command the sons of Israel to observe this day to keep it holy and not do any work on it and not defile it, for it is holier than all other days. And whoever profanes it shall most surely die, and whoever does any work on it shall most surely die eternally, so that Israel's sons may observe this day in every generation and not be uprooted from the land; for it is a holy and a blessed day. . . . Proclaim the law of this day to the sons of Israel and tell them to keep sabbath on it, and not to make the mistake of thinking they can ignore it, and that it is not lawful to do any work that is unseemly or do business on it, or draw water, or carry any heavy load through their gates on it, either in or out, and that they should not prepare on it anything to eat or drink that they have not prepared for themselves already in their homes on the sixth day. And they shall not bring in or take out anything from one house to another on that day . . . And the Creator of all things blessed it, but he did not hallow all peoples and nations to keep sabbath on it, but Israel only. (2:26–31)

Clearly for the author of Jubilees, such care to avoid breach of the sabbath law is part of Israel's responsibility as the people of God. It is a blessing from God which marks them off from all other nations. Similarly, in Chapter 50:

And the man that does any work on it shall die: whoever desecrates that day, whoever lies with a woman, or whoever talks on it about anything he intends to do [what, for example, he will buy or sell next day], and whoever draws water on it because he did not remember to draw it on the sixth day, or whoever lifts any load to carry it out of his tent or out of his house, shall die. You shall do no work whatever on the sabbath day: only what you have prepared for yourselves on the sixth day shall you eat and drink. . . . And any man who does any work on the sabbath days, or goes on a journey or tills a field (whether at home or elsewhere), and whoever lights a fire or loads any beast or travels by ship on the sea, and whoever shoots or kills anything or slaughters a beast or bird or takes an animal or a bird or a fish, or whoever fasts or makes war on the sabbath – the man who does any of these things on the sabbath shall die. (50:8–9, 12–13)

Precisely which group within early Judaism the book of Jubilees speaks for we cannot now tell. We do know, however, that the Damascus Document, probably written about the same time, provided the rulings for the Essene observation of the sabbath. And these are still more strict. In addition to the specific prohibitions of Jubilees, the law against working on the sabbath has been spelled out in still more detail.

No man shall walk abroad to do business on the sabbath. He shall not walk more than one thousand cubits beyond his town. No man shall eat on the sabbath day except that which is already prepared. He shall eat nothing lying in the fields. . . . No man shall willingly mingle (with others) on the sabbath. . . . He shall not open a sealed vessel on the sabbath. No man shall carry perfumes on himself whilst going and coming on the sabbath. He shall lift neither sand nor dust in his dwelling. No foster-father shall carry a child whilst going and coming on the sabbath. . . . No man shall assist a beast to give birth on the sabbath day. And if it should fall into a cistern or pit, he shall not lift it out on the sabbath. No man shall spend the sabbath in a place near to Gentiles on the sabbath. No man shall profane the sabbath for the sake of riches or gain on the sabbath day. But should any man fall into water or fire, let him be pulled out with the aid of a ladder or rope or [some such] tool. (CD = Damascus Document, 10–11)

Here we see, already some hundred years before the ministry of Jesus, the sort of rulings which seem to have characterized much of Pharisaic practice at the time of Jesus. Clearly evident is the same concern to observe the law with total commitment and faithfulness, resulting in a multiplication of rulings, stipulating what it meant truly to observe the sabbath law in a whole sequence of case studies. Already evident is the same concern, as it was put later, to build a fence round the Torah, to ensure that the Torah itself was not infringed, the same concern to mark out the acceptable limits of conduct.

Here again we see Jesus reacting strongly. Two episodes in particular are given prominence in the first three Gospels because they involved controversy with some Pharisees. The first was the occasion when Jesus' disciples were accused of doing "what is not lawful on the sabbath," because they plucked and ate standing grain (Mark 2:23–8). The fault noted, presumably, is the work involved in plucking the ears of grain and preparing to eat them (rubbing off the husks). Even such nominal work was contrary to the repeated and clear rulings in Jubilees and the Damascus Document, that all food consumed on the sabbath should have been prepared on the sixth day. Against such scrupulosity Jesus took a firm stand. It was more important to meet the human need of hunger than to observe the sabbath in such a way (2:25–6). The sabbath was given for human benefit, not to constrain and restrict the meeting of human need (2:27). To make such strict observance of the sabbath a test case for what is acceptable to God is to abuse the sabbath.

The second episode is preserved in close proximity to the first – the episode of Jesus healing the man with a paralyzed hand on the sabbath (Mark 3:1–5). The point again was the lack of urgency in the case. There was no threat to the man's life such as both Essene and Pharisee would recognize as warranting an exception to the law forbidding any work on the sabbath. The man may have been paralyzed for some time; and with the sabbath ending at sunset it would have been quite possible for Jesus to delay his kindly ministrations for a few hours without really disadvantaging the man, and without breaching the sabbath law. But for Jesus the idea that doing a service for someone on the sabbath could be wrong was simply absurd. When sabbath law actually prohibited the doing of good, there was clearly something wrong (3:4). Such attempts to draw with increasing comprehensiveness the lines of what God counted acceptable and unacceptable were misconceived – a basic misunderstanding of what God offered and looked for.

Here again, then, we see Jesus *breaking through the bound-aries* which the religious groups within Judaism at that time were concerned to draw round themselves. The definitions of who were the people of God and what being the people of God required in daily conduct, Jesus saw to be too strict and too tight. The rulings with regard to the sensitive issue of the sabbath had become too restrictive and hurtful to people in need. A greater openness and flexibility was more true to God's intention in providing the sabbath than a rule-book mentality.

Women

One other issue is deserving of comment – not because it occasioned great controversy at the time, but because of its contemporary significance. In the Orient a woman was, and still usually is, regarded as inferior to a man. Her inferiority was emphasized not least in the law. So, for example, it was possible for one man to have several wives (Deut. 21:15–17); but not for one woman to have several husbands. The right of divorce lay wholly in the hands of the husband (Deut. 24:1–4). Women were actually valued at between a half and two-thirds the value of a man (Lev. 27:1–7).

Not least in matters of religion a woman started with a great disadvantage. Where blood was such an important factor as a source of ritual defilement, the woman was naturally "unclean" for much of the time, for seven days after each menstruation (Lev. 12:2). After the birth of a male child the mother was considered unclean for the same length of time; but after the birth of a female child she was unclean for twice as long (Lev. 12:2–5). A normal healthy woman of childbearing age was thus prevented from taking part in religious ceremonies for much of her life. In the eyes of the scrupulous there would always be the danger that she might render others impure by social contact (Lev. 15:19–23). The inferiority was built into the very structure of the temple itself, with the court of women *outside* the court of Israel, with women not even allowed into the inner court where the sacrifices were offered.

It is sufficiently clear that Jesus disregarded these taboos. Women were among his closest followers and friends (Mark 15:40–1; Luke 8:1–3; 10:38–42). The note in John 4:27, that Jesus' disciples were surprised to find him talking alone to a woman in a public place, catches something of the eyebrow-raising unconventionality of his conduct. His teaching on divorce evidently envisaged equivalent rights for both partners (Mark 10:11–12). He was as unconcerned at the possibility of defilement from the woman with the hemorrhage (Mark 5:25–34 – unclean all the time!) as at the possibility of contracting infection from those with contagious skin diseases (Mark 1:40–41). Here again we see the same conviction that *boundaries of acceptability and unacceptability were being drawn too tightly*. Here again we see the same readiness to break through such boundaries, as part of his calling, as part of the good news of God's rule.

In all these cases, therefore, we see Jesus questioning current concepts of what was right, of what showed a person to be accepted by God or to be unacceptable to God, to belong to the people of God or to be outside the scope of God's covenanted grace. In all these cases he was confronted by boundaries drawn *within Israel*, by Jew against Jew, boundaries drawn for religious reasons, drawn by those most admirable for the strength of their commitment in religious matters, those most concerned that their religious practice be what God wants. *In each case Jesus called these boundaries in question, disregarded them, broke them down.* And he did so in the name of God's Kingdom. He came to call sinners, not the righteous. God is for those whom men think to exclude in his name.

A New Motivation

Law and Love

What did all this mean for Jesus' disciples? If the Pharisaic rulings did not provide the pattern for conduct, what did? How should the disciple live? Breaking through the boundaries erected by others is hardly a sufficient program for responsible living. Was the law to be wholly disregarded? That would have been a recipe for total anarchy. If, on the other hand, it was still the law of God, the law of the land, it still needed to be interpreted and applied to the changing circumstances of the present. And if not by Pharisaic-type rulings, how?

In fact Jesus did not call for the law to be abandoned. It was, after all, the civil law as well as the religious law. In a religious state the religious law is the national law. As such it still provided an indispensable framework for life in society. So, for example, the lepers cleansed by Jesus are told to go and show themselves to the priest in order that they might be pronounced officially clean (Mark 1:44; Luke 17:14). And the rich young man, so desirous to ensure his inheritance of eternal life, is reminded of the standards laid down by the commandments (Mark 10:19). Even where Jesus himself interpreted the law in a radical way, it was the law which he so interpreted. The sabbath is still to be observed, but as a gift given for humanity's benefit (Mark 2:27). According to Mark 10:2–9, the Mosaic legislation regarding divorce (Deut. 24:1) is to be interpreted in the light of the prior ordinance of marriage dating back to the creation (Gen 2:24). The law against murder and against adultery is only taken with true seriousness when it is applied also to the hatred and the lust cherished in the human heart (Matt. 5:21–2, 27–8).

In other words, it was not so much the law to which Jesus

objected, as *the way in which it was used.* Not the law itself, but the use of the law as a barrier to exclude others, was what he reacted against; and particularly the overscrupulous interpretation of the law which resulted in a negative judgment against those who failed to conform, the overdefinition of the will of God so that the channels of God's grace became ever more restricted, the attitude which assumed that only what was acceptable to one's own group was acceptable to God.

In place of that attitude Jesus set *love.* Not because he saw love as the opposite of the law – which, after all, gives concrete expression to human responsibility within the covenant relationship – but because he saw love as the key factor in seeking to live in accordance with the law. He summed up the law in the twin command, to love God with all one's heart and soul and mind and strength, and to love one's neighbor as oneself; and he refused to specify any other commandment (Mark 12:28–31). The law was to be obeyed in the light of these fundamental commands, not by subdividing particular commandments into multiple commands. He set forth love of neighbor as *a principle which showed how the law should be observed in the light of circumstances,* rather than as a rule to be obeyed whatever the circumstances. His own life illustrated what this should mean in practice. Love of neighbor in the case of the two sabbath-day incidents, discussed above, indicated the relative unimportance of the various rulings on what was not permitted by the law against sabbath work (Mark 2:23–3:5). The obviously prior obligation of a son to support his parents rendered irrelevant rulings which insisted that the law of vows could not be set aside (Mark 7:9–13). It was *love of neighbor* which breached the taboos and challenged the "us and them" codes of acceptable conduct (Luke 7:39).

It is important to grasp the fact that Jesus did *not* set forth love in place of the law. Nor did he make love itself into a kind of law. For him love was not a demand of discipleship or condition for forgiveness. It was rather the *result* of forgiveness, an expression of gratitude. So it was in the case of the woman who embarrassed Jesus' host by anointing his feet while he was at the meal table. To the critical Pharisee Jesus says, "I tell you, her great love proves that her many sins have been forgiven; where little has been forgiven, little love is shown" (Luke 7:47, New English Bible). So it was with Zacchaeus, whose new love of neighbor, expressed in his readiness to disburse half of his goods to the poor, neither was demanded by Jesus nor was a condition of Jesus' acceptance of him, but was clearly a response to Jesus' own prior offer of acceptance (Luke 19:5–8). This presumably is also the significance of Jesus linking the command to love one's neighbor as second only to the first and great command, to love God with all of one's being (Mark 12:28–31). The one follows from the other. Love of neighbor flows from gratitude to God. Only the experience of being loved to the uttermost enables a love of neighbor which itself endures through all disillusion and setback.

For Jesus two characteristic expressions of such love are *forgiveness* and *service*.

Forgiveness

The love which Jesus called for can be measured by its readiness to forgive. Love of neighbor includes genuine forgiveness of the wrong experienced at the hand of the neighbor. And Jesus clearly saw such readiness to forgive as the mark of discipleship and of the community of disciples.

Then Peter came up to him and said to him, "Lord, how often shall my brother sin against me, and I forgive him? As many as seven times?" Jesus said to him, "I do not say to you seven times, but seventy times seven." (Matt. 18:21–2)

"If your brother sins, rebuke him, and if he repents, forgive him; and if he sins against you seven times in the day, and turns to you seven times, and says, 'I repent,' you must forgive him." (Luke 17:3–4)

That is an astonishing prescription for readiness to forgive. In effect Jesus says that forgiveness must be endless and boundless.

And not just forgiveness of brother is in view. Jesus asked for the same love to be shown not only to the neighbor, but also to the *enemy*.

"You have heard that it was said, 'You shall love your neighbour and hate your enemy.' But I say to you, Love your enemies and pray for those who persecute you, so that you may be sons of your Father who is in heaven." (Matt. 5:43–5)

Such love would inevitably be called on to express itself in forgiveness of that which had made the other an enemy in the first place. The love across boundaries is the forgiveness which wipes the slate clean of wrongs counted and which refuses to cherish memories of hurt received. Of such forgiveness the only adequate model is God's own generosity and grace.

To the exhortation to forgive seventy times seven, Matthew adds a parable ("the Kingdom of Heaven may be compared to . . . ") about forgiveness (Matt. 18:23–35). A servant has been forgiven the immense debt he owed his king. But the same servant refuses to forgive a minor debt owed him by a fellow servant. In consequence the king revokes his original forgiveness and has the ungrateful servant thrown in jail. A parable of forgiveness indeed; but also one of judgment. Forgiveness received should express itself in forgiveness offered. The refusal of forgiveness to another is an indication that forgiveness has not really been accepted. *To refuse forgiveness is to invite judgment.*

To the same effect is the wording of the Lord's Prayer:

Forgive us our debts,
  as we also have forgiven our debtors. (Matt. 6:12)

And Matthew adds the further note of explanation:

For if you forgive men their trespasses, your heavenly Father also will forgive you; but if you do not forgive men their trespasses, neither will your Father forgive your trespasses. (Matt. 6:14–15)

Here again the point is that they only can forgive who have experienced forgiveness. Whereas they who do not forgive thereby demonstrate that they have not received or accepted forgiveness. And this is probably the clue to the puzzle of "the unforgiveable sin" (Mark 3:29). What alone is unforgiveable is the refusal to receive forgiveness, the persistent hardness which shuts out good, and calls white black and good evil (as in Mark 3:22).

Service

For Jesus a second obvious expression of love of neighbor was service of neighbor. In this connection the most striking passage is Mark 10:35–45. The disciples, James and John, think of sharing in God's Kingdom in terms of honor and privilege: "Grant us to sit, one at your right hand and one at your left, in your glory" (10:37). Without denying that such privilege and honor might be granted (10:40), Jesus points in a wholly different direction. The disciple is not forbidden thoughts of greatness; but *the greatness he is pointed to is that of service.* To his disciples Jesus says,

You know that those who are supposed to rule over the Gentiles lord it over them, and their great men exercise authority over them. But it shall not be so among you; but whoever would be great among you must be your servant, and whoever would be first among you must be slave of all. (10:42–4)

The model for the ambitious disciple is not given by the structures of authority and power that characterize the world of politics and business. The model is Jesus himself, Jesus, who put concern for the neighbor's well-being above everything else, above not just social conventions and taboos, but also above possibilities of social advancement and prestige, and even life itself:

For the Son of man also came not to be served but to serve, and to give his life as a ransom for many. (10:45)

To be noted also is the character of this servant-love as outgoing and generous, not calculating and carefully weighed. It was Jesus who, according to Matthew, summed up the law in another working principle for social relationships, what we now call the Golden Rule: "Whatever you wish that other people would do to you, do so to them; for this is the law and the prophets" (Matt. 7:12). His older contemporary, the great teacher Hillel, had made a similar attempt to sum up the law, though in a negative form of the Golden Rule: "That which you hate do not do to your fellows." But for Jesus, the responsibility of love of neighbor was something much more positive, seeking out the neighbor's good, loving your neighbor as yourself.

Jesus illustrates what such neighbor-love might involve in the parable of the Good Samaritan (Luke 10:29–37). Notice who is criticized: the priest and Levite; that is to say, the religious bureaucracy who enable the temple to maintain its function, who keep the religious system of Israel going. The implication is that they refuse even to consider helping the man set upon by robbers because he falls outside their boundaries. He does not fit within their accustomed categories. He cannot be straightforwardly processed. As a dead man, a corpse, he would be a threat to their ritual purity. He would disrupt their life pattern, prevent them exercising the function in which their whole existence as priest and Levite was bound. They refuse to reach across the boundaries which mark out their safe little world. In contrast, the "hero" is a Samaritan, a

member of the despised tribe of racial and religious half-breeds
who now inhabited the territory of the old northern kingdom
of Israel. In choosing such a hero Jesus once again cuts across
the political prejudices and social attitudes, the resentments
and conventions of a hundred and more years. And the neighbor – Who is he? In the story, a nameless individual, without
nation or status specified, someone who needs help from those
who encounter him on the road to Jericho. To love one's neighbor is to respond with generosity across such boundaries.

The call to love one's neighbor as oneself, however, should
not be taken out of proportion. Certainly *the neighbor* is not to
be limited to "the person next door," as the parable makes
clear. The neighbor may be anyone whom I encounter whose
need I can meet. But "anyone" does not mean "everyone." Jesus
does not call for the impossible ideal of loving everyone, even
everyone in need. That would diminish the love I can effectively offer to a matter of mere words, a pious assertion, superficial
and evanescent. That would not be the love enacted by the
Samaritan. Moreover, the love called for is to love the neighbor
"as yourself." Notice again, *"as yourself,"* not *more* than yourself, beyond your personal resources. The *command* is to love
the neighbor with that concentration of effort and resolve
which most often characterizes *self*-love. Jesus does not lay on
his disciples a responsibility which they would find impossible
to bear.

In fact, it is not so much the *demanding* character of servant-
love, which Jesus emphasizes, as its *readiness for unconven-
tional expression*, its willingness to reach out across social
boundaries – its readiness to invite "the poor, the maimed, the
lame, the blind" without thought of return or of repayment
(Luke 14:12–14), its willingness to treat hungry or thirsty or
stranger or naked or sick or in prison as though each was Christ
himself (Matt. 25:40, 45). As we saw in the last chapter, Jesus

was no advocate of violent revolution. But here was a revolution of human relationships more fundamental than most violent revolutions.

In all this Jesus recognizes *the closeknit relationship of love, forgiveness, and service.* For love is forgiveness, the genuine acceptance of the other who has hurt or offended, wronged or slighted. And forgiveness is enabled by the security which comes from the sense of being loved and accepted, not just because of what one is, but in spite of it. And love is readiness to serve, not as a means of gaining favor, of building up a store of credit, but without thought of return. And the readiness to serve stems from and is sustained by the same sense of having received far more than was ever deserved in the first place. Such is the pattern of discipleship and resource for discipleship to which Jesus calls.

Conclusion

(1) Jesus saw his life's work as a mission *to invite sinners*, not righteous to the banquet of God's Kingdom. Like the rich, the righteous have little sense of need. They are secure in their lifestyle and convictions, secure in the confidence of their status and acceptability. Jesus acknowledges that they are unlikely to warm to his message, unlikely to respond. For his message is for sinners, for those who are conscious more of their need, of their unacceptability – not least their social unacceptability, their unacceptability to the righteous.

(2) In thus calling sinners, Jesus *reached across social and religious boundaries.* The "sin" in view was not simply a matter of individual error or breach of moral code. It was a social condition – a failure to live according to the rules of those who defined social acceptability, a failure to measure up to the standards set by the religious elite. Jesus, by his call, by his message

and conduct, calls in question such boundary drawing, whether it is done in terms of social intercourse or of religious festival or of gender.

(3) Moreover, he discouraged his disciples from drawing their own boundaries. The disciple must live by *the principle of love*, love for God and love of neighbor; not by multiplying rules. In the various confrontations preserved in the Gospels, Jesus shows an amazing ability to determine conduct by reference to these first principles. He cuts through the complexities of case-law and precedent, of custom and convention, and illustrates what loving one's neighbor as oneself means in practice. And the Evangelists in turn preserve these accounts, not as new case-law to facilitate the building of a Christian fence around the law, but as illustrations of the spontaneity of a life lived by love.

In short, the discipleship to which Jesus called was a discipleship for sinners, a discipleship which lived through a spirit of thankfulness, a discipleship ready to accept those counted unacceptable by the opinion formers, ready to serve rather than look to be served.

Chapter 5

Would Jesus Have Been Disappointed with the Church?

Jesus proclaimed the Kingdom of God; and, it was the church which came. (Alfred Loisy, *L'Evangile et l'Eglise*, p. 153)

Introduction

So far we have looked at discipleship primarily in terms of Jesus' call to individuals. It was a call which did not defer to wealth and privilege, and which was not determined by religious convention. It was a discipleship of the poor and sinners. At the same time, Jesus' favorite image of the Kingdom of God has a corporate dimension. And the categories of poor and sinners are nothing if they are not social categories. What, then, about *the corporate dimensions of discipleship?* What about the internal dynamics of the group of disciples? How did Jesus expect his disciples to relate to each other? Some of the earlier discussion, of course, overlaps into this area too. Love of neighbor includes, as a special case, love of fellow disciple. Jesus' table-fellowship was a paradigm of mutual relations among the disciples as well as with sinners. To cut across boundaries drawn by others did not mean that the disciples of Jesus were not themselves a recognizable group. What then were its characteristics as a group and in the mutual relationships of disciple with disciple?

The same area of discussion can be approached from another angle. Did Jesus intend to establish the church? Is the church what Jesus wanted? Would he have recognized it? Does "the church which came" match with his expectation of the coming Kingdom of God? In Christian tradition it has been customary to speak of the church as the extension of the incarnation – the Kingdom of God on earth; so that, for example, missionary work was quite naturally understood as an attempt to extend God's Kingdom in the world. And in the evolutionary optimism of a hundred years ago it was easy to assume that biological evolution would naturally continue in moral evolution, that what Jesus meant by the Kingdom of God was a Christian society marked by high moral standards (not unlike Victorian society's self-image!). But the quotation by Loisy at the head of the chapter puts a question mark against such easy optimism. There is more than a hint of surprise and disappointment in it: The church is *not* after all the Kingdom!

Of course the question, Did Jesus intend to establish the church? is poorly framed. For by "church" it is hard to avoid the idea of the church as it has been known down through the centuries – the Churches of Eastern Orthodoxy, the Church of Rome, the Churches of Protestantism, the independent churches, etc. And presumably Jesus did not envisage all that! – especially if he proclaimed the establishment by God of his final rule over all as pressingly imminent. The real question is whether the church as it developed is in line with Jesus' intention. Christianity, after all, stems from Jesus. The Christian church can trace its origins back at least to the events of Easter and Pentecost (Acts 1–2) – Pentecost as the "birthday" of the church. The question, then, is whether this is what Jesus would have wanted. How did what happened in the event match with his expectation of the coming Kingdom of God? Did Jesus intend to establish a community which could develop into what we now recognize as the church?

And even if it may be overambitious to hope for firm answers to such questions, it is still appropriate to ask how the church which has been and is measures up against Jesus' teaching. If Jesus and his teaching provide any kind of paradigm for human relationships, it ill behoves the church to refuse the opportunity of a spiritual check-up here too. Hence the question which forms the title for this chapter – slightly tongue in cheek, but important for all that.

The Community of the New Covenant

One of the major questions in scholarship today is how Jesus saw his vocation in relation to Israel as a whole. Did he see his mission as calling out individuals to live a particular kind of life within Israel? As part of Israel's own vocation as the people of God? To recall Israel to that vocation? Or was his call to Israel as a whole? And would he have been disappointed by the fact that only a relatively small number of his fellow Jews responded? The other groups within Israel at the same time were confronted by the same questions. Were the righteous the only true Israelites? Would the apostate sinners of Israel see the light and acknowledge that the righteous had after all been right and in the end join them? Jesus protested against such boundary drawing; but his own relative lack of success meant that, like it or not, the few who did respond positively formed some sort of group. How did Jesus see this group and its role within Israel, in relation to the Israel of his own day and to the Israel of the future?

Major Considerations

There are several indications that Jesus saw his task, in part at least, as recalling Israel as a whole to its role as the eschatological people of God; or, alternatively, as calling out individuals to constitute the people of God in the new age.

(1) *He chose twelve.* The traditions to this effect are firmly established in the Gospels.

He appointed twelve to be with him, and to be sent out to preach and have authority to cast out demons: Simon whom he surnamed Peter; James the son of Zebedee and John the brother of James, whom he surnamed Boanerges, that is, sons of thunder; Andrew, and Philip, and Bartholomew, and Matthew, and Thomas, and James the son of Alphaeus, and Thaddaeus, and Simon the Cananaean, and Judas Iscariot, who betrayed him. (Mark 3:14–19; so also Matt. 10:1–4 and Luke 6:13–16)

Some have argued that the twelve as such did not emerge as the group round which the church began to cohere until after Pentecost. This is highly unlikely:

(a) To include Judas, the great betrayer, in the circle of Jesus' intimates, if it was not rooted in historical fact, might be counted a very original novelistic touch. But it would have shed a very unfavorable light on Jesus' own perception of the character of those he chose, whereas the mention of Jesus giving surnames to some of his disciples constitutes a claim to precisely such perception. Judas is mentioned not as one whose betrayal Jesus foresaw from the beginning, but as the one who, despite being one of the twelve, in the event actually betrayed him.

(b) The degree of detail retained also indicates very early tradition. For there is no hint that the title "Boanerges" was derived from the character of James and John as exemplified in the early church. Certainly no traditions from the post-Easter period are recalled which would have occasioned the nickname or give it substance. And in the case of the second Simon there may be, in Mark's case at least, something of a cover-up. For he simply transliterates a description ("Cananaean") which would have been more accurately translated "Zealot" (as in Luke 6:15). Here again is the suggestion of a potentially uncomfortable fact (for Mark's readers, Zealot was equivalent to guerrilla) which could be cloaked but not eliminated.

(c) Ironically, the degree of obscurity in the twelve points in the same direction. For between the lists there is some confusion as to who the final members of the twelve were. "Thaddaeus," say Matthew and Mark. "Judas the son of James," says Luke. Add to this that the period of the twelve's leadership of the earliest Jerusalem church does not seem to have been very extensive; it was soon superceded by the leadership of the three pillar apostles (Gal. 2:9), and then of James the brother of Jesus alone (Acts 12:17; 21:18; Gal. 2:12). The consequent implication is that the twelve (as distinct from individual members of the twelve) may not have been so prominent in the early days of the church after all. At least they seem to have been sufficiently unprominent for the memory of who they actually were to have become a little confused!

All of which certainly points to the conclusion that the significance of "the twelve" stems primarily from their role during the ministry of Jesus. The implication is strong that they *did* constitute a group round Jesus, a group who were regarded, by Jesus and others, as particularly "his disciples."

Now the symbolism of twelve is obvious. And it would certainly have been obvious both to Jesus' disciples and to others of the time. For the number twelve must have been chosen as a reflection of the fact that Israel thought of itself as constituted in twelve tribes, descended from the twelve sons of the patriarch Jacob, who was himself named "Israel." For Jesus to choose twelve meant that he intended his twelve disciples to be seen as somehow representative of the twelve tribes, that is, *representative of the people of God* (cf. James 1:1; Rev. 7:4–8; 22:2). In particular we may presume that he intended them as representatives of the eschatological people of God, the Israel of the end time. This is clearly implied in a saying recorded in both Matthew and Luke.

Matt 19:28:	Luke 22:29–30:
Truly, I say to you, in the new world, when the Son of man shall sit on his glorious throne, you who have followed me will also sit on twelve thrones, judging the twelve tribes of Israel.	I assign to you, as my Father assigned to me, a kingdom, that you may eat and drink at my table in my kingdom, and sit on thrones judging the twelve tribes of Israel.

To this must be added the traditions, recalled only in Matthew, that Jesus saw his mission "only to the lost sheep of the house of Israel" (Matt. 15:24), and that he restricted the mission of his disciples similarly to "the house of Israel" (Matt. 10:5–6, 23). The conclusion is hard to avoid, therefore. Jesus directed his ministry to Israel, and saw discipleship in terms of *an Israel faithful to its heritage*, his disciples as representatives of Israel as it should be and will be.

(2) *Sheep and flock metaphors.* One of the metaphors Jesus seems to have delighted in was that of sheep and shepherd. He calls up the familiar image of sheep on a number of occasions (Matt. 7:15; 10:16; 12:11–12). More to the point, he uses the metaphor for his disciples and the recipients of his message.

Fear not, little flock, for it is your Father's good pleasure to give you the kingdom. (Luke 12:32)

As we have just seen, he spoke of his own mission and that of his disciples as only "to the lost sheep of the house of Israel" (Matt. 10:6; 15:24). According to the other of the first three Evangelists, he quoted from Zech. 13:7 shortly before his arrest:

You will all fall away; for it is written, "I will strike the shepherd, and the sheep will be scattered." (Mark 14:27)

In a similar allusion Mark recalls the vivid picture of Jesus disembarking from a boat confronted by the scene of a large crowd scattered and straggling across the hillside. "As he went ashore he saw a great throng, and he had compassion on them, because they were like sheep without a shepherd" (Mark 6:34; similarly Matt. 9:36). And his parable of the lost sheep is recalled by both Matthew and Luke (Matt. 18:12–14; Luke 15:3–7). In John's Gospel the metaphor becomes an extended exposition, in the manner of the Fourth Gospel (John 10:1–30). This use of sheep metaphors for Jesus' disciples is so widespread across the Gospel traditions, it must go back to Jesus himself.

And once again the significance of the image is clear. In the Old Testament, the same image is used regularly for "the flock of Israel" (e.g., Num. 27:17; Pss. 74:1; 79:13; 100:3; Jer. 13:20; Zech. 11:7). Not only so, but it is used to depict the Israel of the new age, Israel restored to God's favor and living fully under God's protection (the kingly rule of God).

> He (God) will feed his flock like a shepherd,
>   he will gather the lambs in his arms,
> he will carry them in his bosom,
>   and gently lead those that are with young. (Isa. 40:11)

Chapter 34 of Ezekiel's prophecy is completely devoted to the theme of Israel as the Lord God's flock: at present under rapacious and harsh shepherds, and now scattered abroad; but soon to be rescued and restored to the good pastures of Israel under God's protection;

And I will set up over them one shepherd, my servant David, and he shall feed them and be their shepherd. . . . And you are my sheep, the sheep of my pasture, and I am your God, says the Lord God. (Ezek. 34:23; cf. Zech. 10:2–12)

Similarly with Micah. Of the coming ruler, from Bethlehem, Micah says:

> He shall stand and feed his flock in the strength of the Lord,
>   in the majesty of the name of the Lord his God.
> And they shall dwell secure. (Mic. 5:4; also 2:12 and 4:6–7).

And the hope continued to be cherished, as we know from the Psalms of Solomon, written less than a hundred years before Jesus' ministry. For there, too, the royal Messiah to come is portrayed as

> Strong in his works, and mighty in the fear of God,
> Shepherding the flock of the Lord faithfully and righteously.
> And he will not let any among them languish in their pasturing.
> (Ps. Sol. 17:44–5)

Here again, then, for Jesus to use the metaphor of sheep and shepherd in the way he did can have only one meaning for us at this point. He saw his mission in terms of these older prophetic hopes. He understood his mission and that of his disciples as an implementation of these hopes, as fulfilling the expectations for Israel in the new age. *They were gathering in the scattered sheep of Israel*, reconstituting the flock of God to be under his protective rule. His contemporaries would certainly have understood his use of that imagery in such terms.

(3) *(New) covenant*. One of the strongest traditions in the early churches' memory of Jesus is that of the last supper – Jesus' last meal with his disciples. It is recalled not only in each of the first three Gospels, but also by Paul, writing about twenty years later and citing an already very old tradition (1 Cor. 11:23–5). The point of relevance here is that in all these versions the last supper is spoken of as a covenant, or new covenant meal.

Matt 26:28/Mark 14:24:	Luke 22:20/1 Cor. 11:25:
This is my blood of the covenant, which is poured out for many.	This cup is the new covenant in my blood, (which is poured out for you).

Whatever the precise wording of Jesus' original utterance, the point for us is the same: Jesus anticipated his death and portrayed it as *a covenant sacrifice.*

Here too no Jew would be in any doubt as to the significance of the imagery. The episode of Exod. 24:3–8 would be recalled.

Moses offered sacrifice to seal the covenant made between God and Israel, the covenant wherein God had bound himself to be their God, and they bound themselves to obey "all the words which the Lord has spoken" (i.e., the law).

And Moses took the blood and threw it upon the people, and said, "Behold the blood of the covenant which the Lord has made with you in accordance with all these words." (Exod. 24:8)

The implication of Jesus' words is that he saw his death as a fresh covenant sacrifice, indicating a fresh, or new covenant between God and God's people. And here again the thought of a new covenant would almost certainly evoke the promise of Jer. 31:31–4, the promise of a new covenant, made by the Lord with the house of Israel, a covenant more appropriate to the new age.

The significance then for those who shared this meal and drank this wine would be profound. As the blood of the covenant sacrifice of old had bound their forefathers and made them participants in the covenant of Sinai, so the blood of the new covenant sacrifice bound the disciples and made them participants in the new covenant. Thus, to partake of Jesus' blood was to express their assent to and part in this new covenant. Theirs is the role of "the house of Israel" in the new age. And as those who took part in the Passover identified themselves with their forefathers of the Exodus and Sinai generation, with whom the covenant had been made, so the disciples identified themselves as the Israel of the end time.

In all these cases the evidence is sound and the implications clear. Jesus did see his task as more than a calling out of scattered individuals. He did see discipleship as having a corporate dimension. Indeed *he saw the disciples as in some sense constituting or representing the twelve tribes of Israel at the end of this age, Israel as the flock of God under the protection of God's kingly rule, the Israel of the new covenant.*

Other considerations, however, are less clear.

Other Considerations

(4) *Did Jesus speak of "the church"*? In any inquiry as to whether Jesus intended to establish the church there are two obvious passages to be cited, both of them from Matthew, both of them words of Jesus.

I tell you, you are Peter, and on this rock I will build my church, and the powers of death shall not prevail against it. (Matt. 16:18)

If your brother sins against you, go and tell him his fault, between you and him alone. If he listens to you, you have gained your brother. But if he does not listen, take one or two others along with you, that every word may be confirmed by the evidence of two or three witnesses. If he refuses to listen to them, tell it to the church; and if he refuses to listen even to the church, let him be to you as a Gentile and a tax collector. (Matt. 18:15–17)

However, considerable doubt must be entertained as to whether these words were spoken by Jesus during his ministry. (a) Both of them are retained only by Matthew. This is not a decisive consideration in itself. (b) But in addition, the first passage looks very much like an elaboration of the earlier, briefer tradition which Mark preserves. In Mark, Jesus' response to Peter's confession is much more ambivalent. And such an interpretative elaboration, to bring out the importance of Peter's confession, would be quite an acceptable way of presenting and passing on the earlier form of the tradition. (c) The second passage looks even more clearly to be an elaboration of the Jesus tradition in the light of the organization which actually did develop, once Jesus was no longer there to arbitrate. And its use of "Gentile and tax collector" with such a negative tone probably expresses the perspective of an early, strongly Jewish, Christian church rather than of Jesus himself (see again Chapter 4). So if we are looking for Jesus' own understanding of his mission, rather than the way that understanding was interpreted and passed down in the different first-century churches, it is less likely that we will find it here.

At the same time, it is worth noticing that the word used for "church" in both passages is the same word as we find regularly in the Greek translation of the Old Testament to denote the assembly of Israel. A good example of this usage comes in Stephen's speech in Acts 7:38, speaking of the Israelite assembly in the wilderness. So the equivalent Aramaic (or Hebrew) word itself could certainly go back to Jesus. Originally it would have meant simply the gathering together of the disciples of Jesus; but with the overtone that these assemblies of Jesus' disciples were the equivalent of the Israelite assembly under the covenant of Sinai. The *"church" is the Israelite assembly of the new covenant.* Here again we see reflected a striking sense of continuity between the first followers of Jesus and the Israel of God.

(5) Equally disputed is the significance of Jesus' expectation of *an imminent coming of the Kingdom of God.* We have already noted this in Chapter 2, and here need simply recall the evidence that Jesus seems to have expected the end of history within the lifetime of his own generation (Mark 9:1; 13:30; Matt. 10:23). The question is obvious: Would Jesus have planned the establishment of a substantial organization if he expected the end to come soon, including the end of such organizations?

If the question is obvious, however, the answer is not. The members of the community at Qumran seem to have been equally convinced that the end of the world would soon be upon them. But that did not stop them from organizing. On the contrary, their organization was in large part directed to preparing them for the crisis of the final end and its sequel. So too, as we shall note later, the early churches thought the return of Jesus would take place very soon. But that hardly stopped them from organizing as churches! So the fact that Jesus saw the end of history, and the final judgment, as imminent would not have prevented him from establishing a community.

On the other hand, the community he had in view was the

community of the new age. The role attributed to the twelve in Matthew 19:28 is that of participation in the final judgment (judging the twelve tribes of Israel). The flock is the flock of Israel, reconstituted under God's own rule after the dispersal which has been a feature of the present age. Talk of the (new) covenant in Jesus' blood goes hand in hand with Jesus' vow not to drink of the fruit of the vine until he drinks it new in the Kingdom of God (Mark 14:25; Luke 22:18). So how much of all this can be simply transferred to a church which continues to be very much of this age, still praying for God's Kingdom to come, is another question.

(6) Most enigmatic of all is Jesus' talk of *a new temple*. Jesus was evidently accused at his trial of saying something of this sort: "I will destroy this temple that is made with hands, and in three days I will build another, not made with hands" (Mark 14:58). In Mark's account this is categorized as a false testimony against Jesus. And presumably the implication is that those who subsequently mocked him in the same terms, while he was hanging on the cross, were equally misinformed (Mark 15:29). But Mark also records Jesus as predicting the destruction of the temple (Mark 13:2). And in John's Gospel Jesus is even recorded as saying something quite like the testimony called false by Mark. "Jesus answered them. 'Destroy this temple, and in three days I will raise it up' " (John 2:19). Moreover, the accusation against Stephen, in Acts 6:14, implies that Stephen too testified that Jesus said something about destroying the temple. So it very much looks as though Jesus did say something about the end of the temple, and probably also about its building again or replacement by a new temple, even if we cannot be sure precisely what it was he did say.

The point for us, of course, focuses on the significance of the temple. It was the cultic center of Israel's whole religion, that around which the whole religion and the whole religious life of the people were organized; particularly in terms of daily and special sacrifices, tithing and the great feasts. To talk of the destruction of the temple was to envisage a radically altered form and pattern of religion, of religious organization and religious life. But to talk of a new temple could mean a new cultic center, a new form and pattern of religion, but equally organized round a temple, a sanctuary where God was present in the midst of his covenant people. Such a vision was by no means strange to many Jews of Jesus' time (cf. e.g., Ezek. 40–8 and the Temple Scroll from Qumran). And even to use the imagery of a "temple," unless in a very transferred sense, was to evoke the image of a highly organized religion and structured form of religious practice. Unfortunately, however, the whole tradition is rather obscure, and we cannot be certain what it was that Jesus did say. So neither can we be quite certain as to what he meant. Did Jesus intend the congregation of the end time to have a cultic center (temple) or some other form of worship which removed the need for such (cf. John 4:21–4; 1 Cor. 3:16; Eph. 2:19–22; 1 Pet. 2:5, Rev. 21:22)?

We are not much further forward, then, than we were after reviewing the major considerations. On the one hand, however, the degree of continuity between the Israel that was and the discipleship to which Jesus called has been reinforced. It was not for a quite different pattern of religion for which Jesus looked, but *a community which would see itself as the fulfilment of Israel's hopes for the age to come.* We will have to explore the implications of this further. But on the other hand, it remains unclear how much of Jesus' vision of community looked to the new age when God's kingly rule would be in full operation, and how much of it can be taken in reference to a church still waiting for the Kingdom to come. If Jesus spoke of a community of the new covenant as the fulfilment of Jewish hopes for the new age, can we in turn speak of the post-Easter churches as the fulfilment of what Jesus held before him? Once again that may be a question more easily asked than answered.

But the asking is nonetheless important, since it at least reminds us that a positive answer cannot be taken for granted.

The more modest task is to attempt to characterize the discipleship of Jesus as it was actually practiced during Jesus' ministry. Whatever his hopes and objectives were, the community of discipleship as it actually existed round him presumably echoed these hopes and objectives in some measure. The pattern of discipleship which the disciples actually experienced presumably influenced them in the way they helped shape the churches which they subsequently founded or of which they were later part. To gain a clearer idea of these characteristics of the disciples' common life should still give us something of a pattern or checklist by which to measure the churches which followed and which, *mutatis mutandis*, are still with us today.

Characteristics of the Community

Jesus called various individuals to follow him. Out of that larger group, including the poor, tax collectors, sinners, and women, he chose a smaller group of twelve. As his disciples, and in his company, he encouraged them to live in accordance with the principal emphases of his own message and conduct: to share their meals in a way which reflected the character of God's kingly rule; to act on the sabbath as those for whom the sabbath had been made; to love, forgive, serve; to see themselves as God's flock, members of the community of the new covenant. What did all this mean for their common life? What was the character of their coming together, their assembly as the Israel of the end time, their structure as "church"?

Centrality of Jesus

One feature stands out at once. It was *a community gathered round Jesus.* Discipleship meant first and foremost following him. The Kingdom he proclaimed was God's Kingdom. But it was Jesus who proclaimed it as present, and as operative in and through his own ministry. The faith he commended in those healed was faith in God's power; but it was that power coming through him. He encouraged his disciples to live before God as children, confident in their Father's provision. But the prayer of intimate family sonship which he taught them (Luke 11:2) was an echo of his own "Abba, Father" prayer (Mark 14:36). As we shall note below, he sent his disciples out on mission. But it was a sharing in his mission, an echoing of his message (Matt. 10:7), a casting out of demons "in his name" (Luke 10:17). Their one attempt to act independently ended in failure (Mark 9:18). In some ways, most striking of all was the choice of twelve. Jesus does *not* count himself as one of the twelve, one of the group representing the Israel of the end time. He stands over against them; they relate to him as the one who appointed them to be "the twelve."

Equally striking is the fact that the twelve are nowhere shown in the Gospel traditions as functioning within the wider group of Jesus' disciples in any kind of hierarchical role. They are closer to him and act as his assistants and missionaries. But they have no intermediary function. All who wish to can come directly to Jesus; and when any try to intervene and regulate, whether the twelve or others, they are regularly rebuked (Mark 9:38–9; 10:13–14; Luke 7:39*ff.*). There is no suggestion of the twelve functioning as "priests" to others' "laity." Discipleship depends directly on Jesus, rather than through others. Even when Matthew includes the tradition of Peter being given power to bind and loose (Matt. 16:19), it is sufficiently clear that, for Matthew, Peter is a representative figure at such points (as again in the other Matthean addition in 14:28–31 – "man of little faith"). And he takes care to include the further tradition of the same power to bind and loose being given to disciples as a whole (18:15–20). Matt. 23 indeed contains very explicit warnings against attempts to claim some kind of intermediate authority, lest it infringe on the authority which belongs to God and to his Christ alone.

You are not to be called rabbi, for you have one teacher, and you are all brethren. And call no man your father on earth, for you have one Father, who is in heaven. Neither be called masters, for you have one master, the Christ. He who is greatest among you shall be your servant; whoever exalts himself will be humbled, and whoever humbles himself will be exalted. (Matt. 23:8–12)

This last is Matthew's version of teaching which Jesus seems to have given on more than one occasion. And again, as with most of the material just reviewed, it probably contains Matthew's interpretative elaboration of the earlier tradition. The temptation to bask in the honor of rank and prestige of title is characteristic of human communities, including the church. But the earlier forms are equally emphatic.

On the way they [the disciples] had discussed with one another who was the greatest. And he sat down and called the twelve; and he said to them, "If any one would be first, he must be last of all and servant of all." (Mark 9:34–5)

The other passage we have already cited in Chapter 4. Jesus rebukes those among his disciples who want a privileged power and authority that sets them apart from and over others.

You know that those who are supposed to rule over the Gentiles lord it over them, and their great men exercise authority over them. But it shall not be so among you; but whoever would be great among you must be your servant, and whoever would be first among you must be slave of all. (Mark 10:42–4)

The pattern for relationships within the community of Jesus' disciples is not the hierarchical model of earthly kingdom or political structure, but a quite different model. Here the values of normal society have been turned completely upside down, and the slave, the lowest level of human society, is given the highest place. here greatness is measured not by authority exercised, but by service rendered. And here once again it is Jesus himself who sets the example for his disciples to follow (Mark 10:45).

In short, *the centrality of Jesus, and the immediacy and directness of the relationship of the disciple with Jesus,* seem to be important features of the community of disciples during Jesus' ministry.

Circles of Discipleship

A second interesting feature is that there seems to have been no real distinction in Jesus' ministry between those who literally followed him and a much wider circle of discipleship which he also recognized. We can speak, indeed, of widening circles of discipleship. Closest to Jesus was perhaps "the beloved disciple" of John's Gospel (John 13:23; 19:26; 20:2). We have to say "perhaps,"for only the Fourth Gospel mentions the beloved disciple, and it is not clear whether he is only a symbol of discipleship or also an anonymous historical individual. But whatever the answer to that conundrum, we can certainly speak of an inner circle of three: Peter, James, and John. A number of occasions are recalled where Jesus seems to have made a point of keeping them close to him, to the exclusion of others (Mark 5:37; 9:2; 13:3; 14:33). And then, of course, there was the circle of the twelve itself, the group whom Jesus had deliberately chosen "to be with him and to be sent out" (Mark 3:14).

In addition, however, we have to speak of a wider circle of disciples, who also literally followed him. Jesus evidently called to discipleship more than the twelve (Mark 10:21, 52; Luke 9:59). Acts 1:23 mentions Joseph Barsabbas and Matthias among those who had been with Jesus since the beginning. And we know of others who went about with him, including women – "Mary, called Magdalene, from whom seven demons had gone out, and Joanna, the wife of Chuza, Herod's steward, and Susanna, and many others" (Luke 8:2–3); "Mary Magdalene, and Mary the mother of James the younger and of Joses, and Salome, who, when he was in Galilee, followed him, and ministered to him; and also many other women who came up with him to Jerusalem" (Mark 15:40–1).

Furthermore, there were disciples who evidently stayed at home. For example, Martha and Mary (Luke 10:38–42; John 11), and the owner of the "upper room" (Mark 14:13–15). They evidently did not see discipleship in terms of an actual following, but were nonetheless disciples. As with the well-to-do women who provided for the disciples "out of their means" (Luke 8:3), discipleship in their case did not require the selling of possessions and the leaving of home. Here too we should include Joseph of Arimathea, "who was also himself looking for the Kingdom of God" (Mark 15:43) and who is called a disciple by Matthew and John (Matt. 27:57; John 19:38 – "but secretly, for fear of the Jews").

Still more striking is the episode where it is recalled that Jesus' mother and brothers came and tried to draw him away from his teaching.

A crowd was sitting about him; and they said to him, "Your mother and your brothers are outside, asking for you." And he replied, "Who are my mother and my brothers?" And looking around on those who sat about him, he said, "Here are my mother and my brothers! Whoever does the will of God is my brother, and sister, and mother." (Mark 3:32–5)

That is a striking redrawing of the boundaries indeed. "Whoever does the will of God," Jesus acknowledges as his family, as linked to him with the closeness of a family bond. *Like the disciple who says "Father," so the one who does God's will belongs within the closeness of Jesus' family circle.*

But Jesus looks still further.

John said to him [Jesus], "Teacher, we saw a man casting out demons in your name, and we forbade him, because he was not following us." But Jesus said, "Do not forbid him; for no one who does a mighty work in my name will be able soon after to speak evil of me. For he that is not against us is for us." (Mark 9:38–40)

The disapproval of the disciples was plain. Here was a man who was outside their circle, and yet acting in the name of their master, without first asking Jesus' approval and enlisting in their ranks. Nevertheless Jesus was willing to let him carry on. He did not forbid the man or require him to become a disciple in some explicit and more formal way. The fact that he was being effective in bringing release to sufferers by using Jesus' name was indication enough that God was honoring his work. And that was sufficient for Jesus. He was willing, in other words, to recognize *a category of discipleship outside the circle of those who had formally declared for him.*

Finally, if we take the emphases of the last three chapters seriously, we may have to recognize a still wider circle of discipleship: the childlike, the poor and the sinners. For, according to Jesus, entry into the Kingdom of God is possible only for those who have turned and become as children. And "whoever humbles himself like this child, he is the greatest in the Kingdom of Heaven" (Matt. 18:3–4). According to Jesus, the Kingdom of God belongs to the poor (Luke 6:20). According to Jesus, the sinner who confesses his need of God's mercy is accepted by God, without any mention being made of a formal discipleship of Jesus (Luke 18:14). Similarly, in the parable of the sheep and the goats, it is the nameless ones of all the nations, the hungry, thirsty, stranger, naked, sick, imprisoned with whom Jesus identifies. "Truly, I say to you, as you did it [not] to one of the least of these, you did it [not] to me" (Matt. 25:40, 45). A wider circle of discipleship there cannot be.

This recognition of the widening circles of discipleship, round Jesus at the center, leads immediately to a third characteristic feature.

Openness

Perhaps the most striking feature of all was *the openness of the community of discipleship*. We can put the point in terms of the previous characteristic. For it is not possible to speak of clear lines of division between these various circles of discipleship; far less of barriers between them. The circles overlapped. Perhaps Mary, the sister of Martha, or Mary Magdalene, was closer to Jesus than some of the twelve. Those "who do the will of God," Jesus acknowledges as belonging to his family. He does not make discipleship consciously embraced as such an essential requirement for acceptance. The disciple must seek (the Kingdom of God) what already in some sense belongs to the poor and the childlike humble.

When we add in the findings of Chapter 4 the point becomes even clearer. Against those who wanted to draw boundaries that kept others out, Jesus protested vigorously. And when disciples attempted to do something the same (as in Mark 9:38), Jesus' response was equally strong. The community of his disciples must *not* see themselves as an exclusive group, as a group who define themselves over against those they keep out. On the contrary, they are a group who by Jesus' characterization are open to the poor and the sinner, to "whoever does the will of God," to "him who is not against us." The "us" of Jesus discipleship is not drawn to exclude "them." It is an inclusive us, open to the outsider, ready to identify us with the marginalized, ready to recognize a community of discipleship, or of God's family, which reaches beyond the more obvious and more formal identity markers.

The contrast with the other religious groupings within Judaism at that time is most marked in the area of *ritual*. As sociologists and anthropologists have long taught us, ritual is one of the ways in which groups express the distinctiveness of their identity, set themselves apart from other groups. And so it was then; two ritual occasions in particular. The first is *baptism* or more generally ritual washings. The disciples of John the Baptist were marked out by the fact that they had submitted to John's baptism. The Essenes at Qumran required a regular discipline of ritual purification for community membership to be sustained. But Jesus made no such demands, practiced no such ritual. It is quite likely that in the earliest days of his mission he, or at least his first disciples, took over the Baptist's own practice (John 3:22, 26; 4:2). But if so, he evidently soon gave it up. Certainly in the major period of his mission, after the Baptist had been put in prison, the point at which the first three Gospels begin their accounts of his mission, there is no mention of baptism. For the bulk of his ministry Jesus seems to have disowned or moved on even from the Baptist's practice. Not even baptism should be a requirement for discipleship. Ritual ablution should not serve as a barrier which the would-be disciple must surmount, and which thereafter marked off "clean" from "unclean." Doing the will of God did not finally depend on such ritual expression.

Secondly, we have already noted the openness of Jesus' *table-fellowship* to tax collectors and sinners. The point is precisely the same here. Jesus' table-fellowship was in no sense a ritual event only for "insiders," a sacramental occasion from which nondisciples were excluded. On the contrary, it was precisely Jesus' openness on this matter which was so offensive. The contrast with Pharisee groups was very striking, since it was by their carefulness on this very point that the Pharisees gained their nickname ("separated ones"). To many Pharisees, Jesus' table-fellowship indicated the casualness of the careless and uncommitted. Whereas, for Jesus, its openness was an integral expression of the good news he had been commissioned to announce.

Jesus seems to have criticized the Qumran community on just this point too. Their ideal of the purity and perfection of the messianic assembly is given in a document listed as the Annex to the Community Rule:

No one who is afflicted with any human impurity may come into the assembly of God. . . . Anyone who is afflicted in his flesh, maimed in hand or foot, lame or blind, or deaf or dumb, or with a visible mark in his flesh, or who is a helpless old man who cannot stand upright in the assembly of the community – these may not enter to take their place in the midst of the community of the men of the name, for the holy angels are in their community. (1QSa 2:3–9)

In contrast, probably pointed contrast, Jesus encouraged his host on one occasion: "When you give a feast, invite the poor, the maimed, the lame, the blind . . . " (Luke 14:13) – the very ones listed prominently in the Qumran list of exclusions. And in the following parable, in which the story of a banquet once again images the Kingdom of God, it is just the same groups whom the servant is urged to bring into the banquet – "the poor and maimed and blind and lame" (Luke 14:21). It is the ritually unacceptable who will participate in the banquet of the Kingdom of God; and the community of the new covenant should express that character of the Kingdom of God in its own common life and table-fellowship.

The openness of Jesus' discipleship, and of the circles of discipleship round him to the still wider circles of discipleship, was one of the most disturbing and challenging features of Jesus' whole ministry. Of course, the wider circles he indicated include many who do not know or own the name of Jesus ("circle of discipleship" is our name for them). Consequently, one of the key tests of the discipleship of Jesus is openness to recognize and acknowledge the reality of the character of such discipleship where no formal profession of discipleship as such is made.

Mission

Two other characteristics of the life shared by the first disciples should be mentioned, for they bear also directly on the understanding of discipleship as a corporate venture. The first is *mission.* According to Mark 3:14 Jesus appointed twelve "to be with him, and to be sent out to preach." The account of his initial summoning of the fishermen brothers, Peter and Andrew, includes the memorable image, "Follow me, and I will make you fishers of men" (Mark 3:19). And the mission of the twelve has a prominent place in the first three Gospels (Mark 6:7–13; Matt. 10; Luke 9:1–6; also 10:1–12). Most striking is the way the commission assumes the dependence of the missionaries on the success (or failure) of their mission. They must carry no baggage or supplies or money. They are to be dependent entirely on the hospitality they are offered in the towns and villages they enter (Matt. 10:9–11). They go forth in the name of Jesus and in the name of the one who sent Jesus (Matt. 10:40). Thus a proof that they are sent by God will be the success of their mission and the provision for their bodily needs. And where they are not received they should move on to the next town (Matt. 10:13–14).

All this is said with reference to the twelve. But within the circles of discipleship we noted that there were those who stayed at home as well as those who literally followed. So in mission there are those who go out in evangelism (the twelve), but not all are evangelists. There are some who must leave behind everything – homes, family, and property (Mark 10:28–9) – to join Jesus in his life as a wandering preacher. But there are others for whom there is a prior obligation to husband or wife (Mark 10:7–9), and whose role in mission is to pray that the lord of the harvest send out laborers into the harvest (Matt. 9:37–8), or to provide the hospitality and back-up for those who go forth. Here again we see the importance of the community dimension of discipleship. In a community not all responsibilities of discipleship devolve on all disciples, or on all disciples alike. And in a community geared for mission, that means a community geared to support those of its members most active in evangelism and mission on behalf of the whole community and of its lord.

Not least of importance here are the sayings which only Matthew has and which may be developed forms of metaphors used by Jesus.

You are the salt of the earth; but if the salt has lost its taste, how shall its saltness be restored? It is no longer good for anything except to be thrown out and trodden under foot by men. You are the light of the world. A city set on a hill cannot be hid. Nor do men light a lamp and put it under a bushel, but on a stand, and it gives light to all in the house. Let your light so shine before men, that they may see your good works and give glory to your Father who is in Heaven. (Matt. 5:13–16)

There is a dimension of mission which is simply that of the testimony of a life lived for God, clear and radiant in the quality of its goodness, a life which brings flavor to what is bland, and preserves the usefulness of what might otherwise go rotten. And this is not just a task for individual discipleship. A "city set on a hill" is an organized community, a community which has set out its position and displays its character clearly in a way that others cannot help seeing. Among its characteristics would be those features highlighted in Chapters 3 and 4.

Thus the character of discipleship as *a community organized to support missionaries reaching out to others with evangelistic urgency* and *to maintain a witness by the very quality of their community life* was there from the beginning. The preservation and adaptation of these Jesus traditions of commission to mission and responsibility for mission show how much they continued to provide a mandate for the first Christians after Easter. No doubt it was this belief in the importance of mission, as well as the open attitude toward participation of others in the new fellowship, which soon resulted in discipleship of Jesus breaching the boundaries that divided Jew from

Gentile. Concern for evangelistic outreach was certainly a point at which the first Christians differed from other Jewish groups and which quickly proved to be a major factor in Christianity's expansion to become a universal religion.

Suffering

It is clear too, however, that Jesus envisaged *suffering* as part of what mission entailed. According to Matthew, Jesus sent out the twelve "as sheep in the midst of wolves" and warned them to be prepared for arrest and persecution, for betrayal and misrepresentation:

They will deliver you up to councils, and flog you in their synagogues, and you will be dragged before governors and kings for my sake, to bear testimony before them and the Gentiles. . . . Brother will deliver up brother to death, and the father his child, and children will rise against parents and have them put to death; and you will be hated by all for my name's sake. . . . When they persecute you in one town, flee to the next. . . . It is enough for the disciple to be like his teacher, and the servant like his master. If they have called the master of the house Beelzebul, how much more will they malign those of his household. (Matt. 10:16–25)

Such is the character of the discipleship to which Jesus called. Jesus describes it as part of the blessedness of being a disciple, a matter for rejoicing since such persecution was confirmation that disciples were heirs of the prophets (Matt. 5:11–12; Luke 6:22–3). The way of discipleship is the way of the cross. "If anyone would come after me, let him deny himself and take up his cross and follow me" (Mark 8:34). The only person who "takes up his cross" is the condemned man carrying it to the place of execution!

In all this the first Christians never forgot that Jesus himself was the paradigm. His life and ministry had ended in the death of the cross. This was what his proclamation of the Kingdom and living his life under God's kingly rule had come to. This too was an expression of the life of the Kingdom. Acceptance of the outsider brought on his head the wrath of the insiders. And though the first Christians naturally rejoiced that he had risen from the dead, teachers like Paul never allowed them to forget that the way into the Kingdom passed through many tribulations (Acts 14:22), that only those who shared in Christ's death would also share in his resurrection (e.g., Rom. 8:17).

Marks of the Church?

These then are some of the characteristics of the community of Jesus' disciples as Jesus envisaged it, and as the earliest churches tried to practice it in at least some measure. But other "marks of the church" have been indicated at different points in the discussion of this chapter. In concluding this study of the communal character of discipleship of Jesus, therefore, it is appropriate to highlight a few of them – further threads in a pattern of church, further elements in a possible "checklist" by which to check how far any body claiming to be a church of Jesus measures up to the discipleship to which he called. Here are four.

(1) *Continuity from Israel.* We cannot do justice to the consistent emphasis which emerged from our first line of inquiry in this chapter without giving this consideration prominence. Jesus saw his disciples as representing the people of the new covenant, the reconstituted flock of Israel. He had no thought whatsoever of founding a new religion. Certainly he is shown as concerned for Samaritans and Gentiles whom he encountered; but it is a share in the bounty of Israel which he offers them (Matt. 15:24–8; John 4:22). And even when a mission to the Gentiles became a prominent feature of the early churches' life, this perspective of Jesus was never lost sight of. Paul, the greatest apostle to the Gentiles, insists that the Gentile Christians are like wild olive branches which have been grafted onto

the olive tree of Israel (Rom. 11:17–24). The ecclesiology is clear and consistent. The church of Jesus Christ is a form of Judaism. Disciples of Jesus are Jews of the new covenant. The church is the eschatological assembly of Israel.

(2) *A one-generation church.* Jesus' expectation of the imminent coming of the Kingdom of God is usually taken as a problem for Christians and theologians. The Kingdom he announced has not come! His disciples still pray for its coming. "Jesus proclaimed the Kingdom; and it was the church which came." But there is another aspect to it which is usually ignored – the fact that Jesus saw discipleship in terms of a single generation. He did not see the need for an organization and structure which went beyond a single generation. Here again the first churches in fact were a true echo of Jesus' own perspective. For they too thought that the end of history would soon be upon them, with the coming again of the exalted Jesus (e.g., 1 Thess. 4:15–17). The mission instructions which they made their own operated within a similarly short-term horizon (Matt. 10:7–10). They too did not think of a church which had to plan its organization and structure to last into future generations. After the centuries of highly organized Judaism, this shortness of planning perspective was presumably one of the most liberating and exhilirating features of this discipleship of Jesus. The same perspective was also part of its openness, since it did not impose formal structures on others who responded positively to Jesus or who sought to do God's will in ways which fell outside the more traditional structures.

(3) *Family.* Jesus saw his circle of disciples as a new family. Those who did the will of God were his brother and sister and mother (Mark 3:35). Those who had left house or brothers or sisters or mother or father or children to follow him would find they had gained a much wider family of brothers and sisters, mothers and children (Mark 10:29–30). The encouragement to live before God as Father, with the implicit trust of a child

confident in his or her father's protection and provision (Matt. 7:7–11 etc.), carries the same implication. What is envisaged is not a set of merely individual relationships. The child–disciple has brothers and sisters. The prayer they were taught as a mark or privilege of their discipleship (the Lord's Prayer) is a communal prayer (Matt 6:9–13; Luke 11:1–4). This instinct and insight was also carried over into the earliest churches in the continued use of the "Abba, Father" prayer, the understanding of Christians as fellow heirs with Christ, and in the recognition of each other as "brothers," with Christ himself as the elder brother (as in Rom. 8:15–17, 29; 1 John 3:11–18). A similar emphasis on the family character of discipleship derives from the importance of table-fellowship for Jesus and the first Christians. One of the most characteristic images in all that has been studied above is the meal table, with the family of disciples gathered round, enjoying each others' company, and with Jesus as the host.

(4) *Diversity of ministry.* Jesus put forward a pattern of discipleship characterized by service (Mark 10:42–4). We may say that he took seriously the word we translate *ministry.* "Ministry" was what the metaphor indicated – service, the activity of one who serves others, who waits on others. For Jesus this was wholly different from a concern for hierarchical government and the power and authority of rule. But his recognition, as we may say, of different "circles of discipleship" included also a recognition of different patterns of service and ministry. Some literally followed him, left home, engaged in mission, and depended on the support of others. Some stayed at home, and their ministry was in financial support and in prayer that the lord of the harvest might send forth laborers into the harvest. Some no doubt found that doing the will of God meant for them faithful service in the vocation, from which Jesus did *not* call them away. And some in seeking to help the poor and needy did not even know that they were doing it as to Christ.

This too was a point not lost on the early churches, where in particular the image of the church as the body of Christ underlined the fact that unity of church depends on diversity of ministry (1 Cor. 12).

Such were some of the marks of the eschatological assembly of Israel as Jesus held it forth before his disciples and as they tried to practice it when Jesus' earthly presence was no longer with them.

Chapter 6

Concluding Reflections

Summary

In this study we have focused on discipleship of Jesus in a quite specific sense: the discipleship to which Jesus himself actually called his hearers during his ministry in first-century Palestine. The outlines of that call and of the discipleship to which he called are clear.

(1) *It begins from God and focuses on God.* God's rule as Creator and as the one who alone can command allegiance and accountability from all created beings is the primary motive for discipleship. The call is primarily for life and living to be oriented entirely in accordance with that fact – to seek first the Kingdom of God. It is an urgent call: To delay might be not only dangerous, but fatal.

The discipleship to which Jesus called also turned upside down the social and religious conventions of his day.

(2) *It gave first place to the poor* ("pride of place" would distort the emphasis). The Kingdom of God is theirs! Not as something which can be imposed or fully implemented in this age; but as a recognition of God's priorities, in contrast to those of human society, and as an enabling to live and work within the structures and relationships of this age in the light of these priorities.

(3) *It gave equal first place to sinners* – those marginalized or even excluded from the circle of God's favor by the righteous. Jesus' call to discipleship is a permanent warning against any form of discipleship which exists by drawing tight definitions

121

and strictly controlled practices round it as a barrier cutting itself off from others. His discipleship is rather to be characterized by the outgoing love, acceptance, and service which marked his own ministry.

(4) Not least it was a discipleship which *reaffirmed Jesus' own heritage,* even while opening it to wider circles. His concern was that his fellow Jews should participate in the full blessings of God's covenant promises for Israel. But the resulting community of discipleship should be an extended family, open to all who seek to do God's will. It should be prepared to share his mission, and his suffering. And it should beware of the danger of conforming its structure and relationships to the pattern of the institutions of this age. In this, as in other matters, Jesus himself provides the primary role model.

The Other Side of Easter

But how relevant is all this to would-be disciples of the late twentieth century? A focus so exclusively on the three years of Jesus' ministry in first-century Palestine surely makes the whole matter much more remote to today. The outlines of the discipleship to which Jesus called more than nineteen-and-a-half centuries ago are clear enough. But today there is no Jesus who walks into butchers' shops, or accountants' offices, or school classes to say "Follow me," in the expectation that those called will literally leave everything behind and follow him in the way of discipleship.

Apart from anything else, there is the difference made by Good Friday and Easter Day, not to mention Pentecost. That means that Jesus is no longer with us, at least in the physical body which made possible a literal following. But it also meant that the message of the first disciples shifted in focus, from Jesus' proclamation of the Kingdom of God to the disciples' proclamation of Jesus, his death and resurrection, and the consequent offer of the gift of the Spirit. So, does not the focus and character of discipleship also shift? And should a study of Jesus' call to discipleship not extend to the earliest Christians' proclamation of the Gospel, and include also the character of the post-Easter, post-Pentecost Christian communities, if it is to have any hope of speaking to us who are also on the other side of Easter?

All this is true, and a more comprehensive study of discipleship in the New Testament as a whole would require a much fuller treatment and allow a more careful study of the central importance of Good Friday, Easter, and Pentecost in any understanding of Christian discipleship now. Nevertheless, the more narrowly focused study just completed retains its value. It remains important to gain as clear a picture as possible of the discipleship to which Jesus called his first disciples in its own right, and not simply as a subsection of a larger profile dominated by the post-Easter perspective.

For one thing, as noted in the first chapter, *any doctrine of the incarnation and any concern to root Christian faith in history must regard the ministry of Jesus on earth as a matter of supreme interest and significance.* How Jesus spoke and acted within the social structures and human relationships of everyday life is bound to provide some sort of definitive paradigm or principles for his followers, however much that paradigm or those principles were conditioned by time and culture.

For another, as we noted at the end of Chapter 4, *Jesus himself remained central in post-Easter discipleship.* Indeed, we may say that this was one of the primary reasons why the first Christians began to practice baptism after Pentecost, although Jesus himself had abandoned John the Baptist's practice during his own ministry. The most significant difference between the Baptist's baptism and that of the first Christians is that the latter was baptism "in the name of Jesus" (Acts 2:38; 8:16; 10:48; etc). And as 1 Cor. 1:12–15 clearly implies, baptism in the name of someone was understood to mean becoming that someone's follower, a member of his party. In other words, baptism "in the name of Jesus" from the beginning took the place of the earlier response to Jesus' own call to "Follow me." Those who were baptized by the first believers were thereby responding to the same call to discipleship, to follow him and learn of him as had the disciples during Jesus' own ministry.

And for another, the memory of that earlier discipleship, of Jesus' teaching on discipleship and what it involved, remained of primary significance for the post-Easter communities. This was why these memories were circulated and treasured and within a generation began to be collected and written down, to form over a few decades our Gospels. Of course they recalled these memories in the light of Good Friday, Easter, and Pentecost. But they did not discard them as no longer relevant to post-Easter discipleship. On the contrary, the Gospels are designed precisely to provide a framework in which that pre-Easter ministry can be retained because of its continuing value to would-be disciples. Much if not most of the Gospel traditions will have taken their present form precisely as catechetical teaching – instruction for new converts on the life of discipleship, material which documents the principles and illustrates the quality of action and relationship which should characterize the disciple and the community of disciples.

What we have done in the present study, therefore, is the twentieth-century equivalent of what Christian teachers will have done with the Gospel traditions from the beginning. We have taken the Gospels as teaching material for Christian discipleship in the here and now. In proper twentieth-century manner we have been concerned to illuminate the Gospel traditions by setting them as fully as possible within the historical context of the time. But the concern has been the same as it will have been in the use of the Gospels for nineteen centuries: to provide instruction, illumination, and inspiration for the life of discipleship in the present.

Jesus' Call to Discipleship Today

How then, in conclusion, can we bring out the continuing importance of the findings of this study? The findings themselves have been summarized at the end of each chapter, and readers should refer back to these concluding sections of Chapters 2–5. Here I will simply draw attention to the larger principles which seem to emerge and to underlie the more specific findings.

The discipleship to which Jesus called was *practical and not merely theoretical.* "The Kingdom of God" may seem to us today an issue for discussion at the level of academic theology more than a factor affecting daily living. But it certainly was not so then, and should not be so now, however we may attempt to translate it into categories and terms which speak more directly to the different and diverse societies of the late twentieth century. In Jesus' case it provided the motivation for his ministry. It came to concrete expression in the healing of the sick, in the reaching out to the poor, in the practicality of whom you eat your daily bread with. A discipleship which allows itself to become absorbed in theoretical debate and which does not come to expression in such practicalities of everyday life is at some remove from the discipleship of Jesus.

The discipleship for which Jesus called was *social and not merely spiritual.* It was not political in the sense that it saw its primary purpose as changing the political or economic system. But neither was it apolitical in the sense that it simply accepted the social structures and conventions of the day and either ignored them or operated within them. Jesus very deliberately challenged several of these social structures and conventions.

He affirmed in word and deed God's favor for the poor – a theme hallowed, of course, in the Torah and the Prophets (the Old Testament theology of poverty), but one too easily and too often set aside in the harsh economic realities of the time. He lived out his message in such a way as to call into radical question the taboos and rules which governed social relationships and determined religious status. In a religious state such a policy was dynamite! The result, not surprisingly, was the same as if he had pursued a much more explicitly political or military policy. In a century familiar with a distinction between social gospel and spiritual gospel this dimension of Jesus' ministry dare not be neglected.

The discipleship to which Jesus called was *corporate and not merely for individuals.* Discipleship was not merely a matter of what the individual did with his or her aloneness before God. The new covenant, like the old, had a horizontal as well as a vertical dimension. It called for love of neighbor as well as for love of God. The two went together, and the latter could not be professed without the former, just as the former could not be sustained without the latter. Here again important traditions within historic Christianity have too often overemphasized the one-to-one relationship between God and the Christian, at the expense of the Christian's responsibility to fellow Christians and to the broader society. But for Jesus, discipleship meant belonging to the flock of Israel, to the new family of those who sought to do God's will as their first priority, to those who celebrated the Kingdom of God in the company of the meal table. Jesus' call to discipleship involves and demands participation in the life of God's new people.

The discipleship for which Jesus called was *both open and committed.* For many people today, Christians included, these two are a contradiction in terms. For them it is impossible to be both open and committed: The open are not sufficiently committed; the committed cannot be really open. Jesus shows that this simply need not be so. There can be no question of the commitment his whole ministry displayed. But neither can there be any question about his openness to the "outsider" and the "irreligious." And he expected no less from his disciples: the commitment of discipleship, to make the Kingdom of God and the will of God the absolutely top priority; but also the openness to those others who did good even though not registered disciples, or who expressed their discipleship in different ways. Indeed, we might say that one of the tests of the discipleship to which Jesus called was the readiness to recognize that there are different patterns and circles of discipleship. Only those who are not really secure in their own discipleship feel it necessary to attack the claims of others to discipleship. It is the refusal to offer forgiveness and acceptance to others which attests a failure fully to accept and live out of the forgiveness of God.

The discipleship of Jesus had *an integrally charismatic character.* It was not tightly structured or marked by detailed planning. The openness to others was also an openness to the prompting of the Spirit and to the demands of the occasion. The first disciples left everything to follow him. But others continued in their familiar jobs and routines ready to provide for those who literally followed. Jesus' criticism of the Pharisees over the Sabbath was a criticism of an attitude which looked first to precedent and rulebook and only then to the person in need. Mission meant a readiness to stay and a readiness to leave, depending on how the message was received. The imminence of the Kingdom meant that discipleship could be stripped to the bare necessities, itself a reminder that the people of God are a pilgrim people, with no enduring stake in this present age. In a day when the weight of 1,900 years of tradition and multimillion-dollar investment in property often seem to overwhelm everything else in the older Christian Churches, in a day when the complexity of modern living can become an excuse to justify almost anything as an expression of discipleship, it is important to remember the starker simplicities of Jesus' first call, "Follow me."

Selected Bibliography

Beasley-Murray, G. R., *Jesus and the Kingdom of God* (Grand Rapids: Eerdmans / Exeter: Paternoster, 1986). The most recent full-scale treatment of Jesus' teaching on the subject.

Cassidy, R. J., *Jesus, Politics, and Society. A Study of Luke's Gospel* (Maryknoll, N.Y.: Orbis, 1978). This study of the profoundly revolutionary character of Jesus' teaching has won widespread praise.

Chilton, B., and McDonald, J. I. H., *Jesus and the Ethics of the Kingdom* (London: SPCK / Philadelphia: Westminster, 1987). A recent attempt to demonstrate the ethical outworkings of Jesus' teaching on the Kingdom of God.

Dunn, J. D. G., *Unity and Diversity in the New Testament. An Inquiry into the Character of Earliest Christianity* (London: SCM / Philadelphia: Westminster, 1977; 2nd ed. 1990).

Dunn, J. D. G., *The Evidence for Jesus. The Impact of Scholarship on Our Understanding of How Christianity Began* (London: SCM / Philadelphia: Westminster, 1985).

Dunn, J. D. G., "Pharisees, Sinners, and Jesus," *The Social World of Formative Christianity and Judaism. Essays in Tribute to Howard Clark Kee*, ed. J. Neusner et al. (Philadelphia: Fortress, 1988) pp. 264–88; reprinted in Dunn, *Jesus, Paul, and the Law* (London: SPCK / Louisville: Westminster, 1990), Chapter 3. The technical study behind the more popular treatment of Chapter 4.

Dunn, J. D. G., ed., *The Kingdom of God and North-East England* (London: SCM, 1986).

Hengel, M., *Property and Riches in the Early Church* (London: SCM, 1974). Hengel, M., *The Charismatic Leader and His Followers* (Edinburgh: T. & T. Clark, 1981). Hengel's unsurpassed knowledge of the ancient world at the time of Jesus and his ability to boil that information down to ordinary-mortal-size bites are well illustrated in these two quite brief studies.

Hoppe, L. J., *Being Poor. A Biblical Study* (Wilmington, Del.: Glazier, 1987). A popular but thorough study of the most important biblical material.

Lohfink, G., *Jesus and Community. The Social Dimensions of Christian Faith* (Philadelphia: Fortress / London: SPCK, 1985). The best nontechnical treatment of the questions, Did Jesus found a church? and, What kind of community did Jesus seek to promote?

Jeremias, J., *New Testament Theology. Vol. One: The Proclamation of Jesus* (London: SCM, 1971). Despite being challenged at several points and some overstatement, this still remains the best detailed and technical attempt to uncover the principal themes of Jesus' preaching.

Meyer, B. F., *The Aims of Jesus* (London: SCM, 1979). Next to Jeremias, this continues to be the best overall treatment of Jesus' objectives and teaching.

Schrage, W., *The Ethics of the New Testament* (Philadelphia: Fortress / Edinburgh: T. & T. Clark, 1988). The most recent thorough treatment of the subject, aiming to clarify the central ethical concerns and their theological basis, of Jesus as well as of each of the NT authors.

Segovia, F. F., ed., *Discipleship in the New Testament* (Philadelphia: Fortress, 1985). Technical and provocative studies on the theme of discipleship in each of the Gospels and in several of the other NT writings.

Questions for Discussion

Chapter 2

1. What meaning has talk of "the Kingdom of God" today? Is there an alternative image or concept which would be more meaningful to people living in the late twentieth century?
2. In what sense can we say that "the Kingdom of God" was present or active in Jesus' ministry? What are Christians praying for when they say the Lord's Prayer: 'Thy Kingdom come'?
3. Can we "build" God's Kingdom (for example, by our giving), or "extend" God's Kingdom (for example, by social, political or evangelistic means)? What is the relation of God's Kingdom to the church(es) and to society?
4. Is repentance necessary to discipleship? In what ways might it express itself in today's world?
5. How can people today "follow" someone who lived 2,000 years ago? How can trust in God and human responsibility be practiced together?

Chapter 3

1. How would you define "poverty" as spoken of in the Bible? Is it possible to be both rich and "poor"? What are the dangers of being "poor," and the dangers of wealth? What relation has material well-being to "salvation"?
2. What does it mean to speak of God as "God of the poor," or

as biased to the poor? What responsibility toward the poor do the Bible and the Gospel lay upon the well-to-do?

3. Is such responsibility purely an individual affair (what each does with his/her surplus)? And does it extend only to the less well off within your own community? Or does such responsibility require cooperative, social, and/or political action? And does it extend to the poor of other nations?

Chapter 4

1. Who are the "sinners" and "righteous" today? In what group would you place yourself or your group? Really? Why?

2. Why was table-fellowship such an important factor in defining who was acceptable and who was not? Is there an equivalent to table-fellowship, either as excluding or as open to the unacceptable, in today's churches?

3. What lessons do the sabbath controversies of Jesus, and Jesus' relationship with women, hold for discipleship today?

4. What tensions between law and love exist in our communities? Are there sufficient opportunities for the offering and receiving of forgiveness in churches today?

5. How can we translate love of neighbor into practice in modern society? Who would provide an example of "the good Samaritan" today?

Chapter 5

1. Did Jesus direct his mission to Israel? To Israel as a whole? In what sense, if any, is Christianity "the new Israel"? How should Jews and Christians regard each other?

2. What are the characteristic "marks" of the church by

which the church may be recognized to be the church? Put them in order of priority and importance.

3. Does the community of discipleship exist for itself or for others? What does your answer mean in practice? What should it mean in practice?

4. What does "outside the church" mean from the perspective of God or of Jesus? How may the openness of Jesus' discipleship be translated into the different situations of today?

5. What does the centrality of Jesus and of the example he gave say about the idea and practice of ministry in the churches of today?

Index

SUBJECTS AND NAMES

Abraham, 26

Beatitudes, 35–6, 52–3
believe, *see* faith

church, 92–4, 101–2; continuity
with Israel, 117–18, 122; as
family, 118–19; one generation,
118
covenant, new, 94–100

discipleship: circles of, 108–13; and
mission, 113–16; openness of,
111–13; and suffering, 116–17;
today, 125–8

exorcisms, 11, 16

faith, 25–30, 31
freedom, 58–9

Jesus: centrality of, 105–8, 123–4;
impact of, 1–2; and law, 83–5;
parables of, 17, 88–9; possibility
of historical knowledge
concerning, 3–4; and Sabbath, 80–
1, 83; and sinners, 70–6, 90;
table-fellowship of (*see* table-
fellowship); and women, 81–2
John the Baptist, 14, 22, 34–5, 112
judgment, final, 55

Kingdom of God, 6–10, 92–4, 106,
121; belongs to poor, 35–6, 44–54,
59–60; imminence of, 13–19, 30–
1, 54–6, 102–3; presence of, 11–
13, 30, 53–4, 105

Last Supper, 99–100
law, 64–6, 83–5, 88; *see also*
Sabbath
love of neighbor, 83–90, 91

Martha and Mary, 109
Ministry, diversity of, 119–20
Mission, 113–16

Pharisee(s), 16, 69, 74–6, 112; and
Sabbath, 79–81
poor, the, 33–44, 53–4, 105, 110,
121; good news for, 52–9;
theology of, 39–44, 59–61

Qumran community, 49–50, 69, 74–
5, 112–13

repentance/conversion, 19–25, 31

sabbath, 76–81, 105
sinners, 62–70, 105, 110, 121;
apostates as, 67–8; Gentiles as,
66–7; and Jesus (*see* Jesus); and
righteous, 68–72; sectarian use of
term, 68–70

table-fellowship, 11–12, 72–6, 105,
112

135

Tax-collectors, 62–3, 68, 101
Temple, new, 103–4
Twelve, the, 95–7, 106–7, 114

wealth, dangers of, 56–8, 59
women, 81–2, 105

Zacchaeus, 22
Zealots, 45–7

SCRIPTURAL REFERENCES

Old Testament

Genesis
  2:24   83
  15:6   26
Exodus
  20:2   65
  24:3–8   99
  24:8   100
  31:12–17   77
Leviticus
  4–5   20
  12:2–5   81
  12:2   81
  15:19–23   81
  27:1–7   81
Numbers
  27:17   98
Deuteronomy
  10:16   20
  15:7–11   40
  21:15–17   81
  24:1–4   81
  24:1   83
  24:10–15   40
  24:19–22   40–1
Joshua
  7   65
2 Samuel
  12:1–6   38
1 Kings
  21   38

Job
  5:16   39
Psalms
  1:1–2   64
  9:17   67
  9:18   39
  10:12–14   39
  12:5   43
  14:6   43
  24:7–10   7
  28:3   64
  34:6   39
  55:2–3   64
  68:5   43
  74:1   98
  79:13   98
  100:3   98
  104:35   64
  113:7   43
  119:53, 155   64
Proverbs
  13:8   37
  14:20   37
  18:23   37
  19:4   37
  23:21   37
  28:19   37
  30:8–9   37
Isaiah
  3:14–15   41
  24:21–2   11
  25:6–9   12
  29:18   11, 35
  29:20   35
  35:4   35
  35:5–6   11, 35
  40:11   98
  43:10   26
  55:7   20
  56:1–7   77
  56:4–5   77
  56:4   77
  56:6–7   77
  56:6   77
  58   20

58:3, 6–7	42
61:1–2	35
61:1	11, 35, 36
61:2	35
Jeremiah	
3:12, 14, 22	20
13:20	98
31:31–4	100
Ezekiel	
34:23	98
40–8	104
Daniel	
1:8–16	73
2:34–5	11
4:34	7
7:27	11
Amos	
2:6–7	42
8:4–6	42
Hosea	
6:1	20
Micah	
2:12	98
4:6–7	98
5:4	98
Zechariah	
10:2–12	98
11:7	98
13:7	97

New Testament

Matthew	
3:7–12	35
5:3	36, 52
5:11–12	116
5:13–16	115
5:21–2	83
5:23–4	50
5:25–6	17, 55
5:27–8	83
5:33–7	59
5:38–44	47
5:43–5	86
5:46–7	68

5:47	67
6:9–13	119
6:12	86
6:14–15	87
6:19–21	56, 58
6:24	56, 58
6:25–34	58
6:25, 27	58
6:28–33	29
6:31	58
7:7–11	28, 119
7:12	88
7:15	97
7:19	55
7:24–7	14
7:26–7	55
8:8–9	28
8:9, 10	28
8:11	9
9:36	98
9:37–8	114
10	114
10:1–4	95
10:5–6	97
10:6	97
10:7–10	118
10:7	6, 106
10:9–11	114
10:13–14	114
10:16–25	116
10:16	97
10:17–22	56
10:23–5	8, 57
10:23	18, 97, 102
10:28	13
10:29–31	29
10:34–6	23
10:37	23
10:39	55
10:40	114
11:1–6	16, 34
11:3–5	51
11:3	34
11:4–5	35
11:5	11, 35

Matthew (*cont.*)
11:12	8
11:19	14, 62, 72
11:20–4	16, 55
11:21	21
11:25	30
12:11–12	97
12:27	11
12:28	11, 51
12:33	22
12:41	21
12:43–5	21
13:16–17	12, 51
13:24	6
13:31, 33	6
13:44–6	9
13:44, 45, 47	6
13:53–8	33
14:28–31	106
15:22–7	28
15:24–8	117
15:24	97
15:28	28
16:18	101
16:19	106
16:24–5	23
17:24–7	50
18:3–4	110
18:3	9, 21, 24, 59
18:8–9	55
18:8	13
18:12–14	98
18:15–20	106
18:15–17	101
18:21–2	85
18:23–35	86
19:28	97, 103
20:21	9
21:31	63
23	106
23:8–12	107
23:16–22	59
23:26	22
24:43	17
24:45–51	17
25:1–12	17
25:40	89, 110
25:41–6	57
25:45	89, 110
26:28	99
25:57	109

Mark
1:1	36
1:4	20
1:14–15	6
1:14	25
1:15	8, 14, 21, 25, 30, 34
1:40–1	82
1:44	83
2:5	51
2:16	62, 72
2:17	62, 70, 71
2:18–19	12
2:19	14, 51
2:23–3:5	84
2:23–8	80
2:25–6	80
2:27	80, 83
3:1–5	80
3:4	80
3:14–19	95
3:14	108, 114
3:19	114
3:20–30	16
3:22	87
3:27	11
3:29	87
3:32–5	109
3:35	118
4:26–9	9
4:40	28
5:25–34	82
5:27–8	28
5:34	28
5:36	27
5:37	108
6:1–6	33
6:2	34
6:7–13	114
6:34	98

7:1–23	75	14:36	106
7:8	75	14:41	67
7:9–13	84	14:58	103
7:14–23	75	15:1, 10, 15	67
8:34–5	23	15:26	46
8:34	116	15:29	103
9:1	17–18, 102	15:40–1	82, 109
9:2	108	15:43	109
9:18	106	**Luke**	
9:23	27	3:10–14	22
9:34–5	107	4:17–21	33, 34
9:38–40	110	4:18	62
9:38–9	106	4:25–7	34
9:38	11, 111	5:29	72
9:47	9	6:13–16	95
10:2–9	83	6:15	46, 95
10:7–9	114	6:20	32, 35, 44, 52, 110
10:11–12	82	6:22–3	116
10:13–14	106	6:32–4	68
10:15	8	6:33	67
10:17–31	21	7:36	72
10:19	83	7:37	62
10:21–2	22	7:39ff.	106
10:21	108	7:39	16, 62, 84
10:28–9	114	7:47	85
10:28	23	7:48	51
10:29–30	118	7:50	28
10:35–45	87	8:1–3	82
10:37, 40	87	8:2–3	109
10:42–4	87, 107, 119	8:3	60, 109
10:45	88, 108	9:1–6	23
10:47–8	28	9:16	72
10:52	28, 108	9:23–4	23
11:22–4	28	9:59–60	15
12:28–31	84, 85	9:59	108
13:2	103	9:61–2	15
13:3	108	10:1–12	114
13:24–30	18	10:4	15
13:30	102	10:9	6
13:34–6	17	10:17	106
14:13–15	109	10:29–37	88
14:24	99	10:30	45
14:25	103	10:38–42	82, 109
14:27	97	10:38	72
14:33	108	11:1–4	119

Luke (cont.)
11:2	8, 106
11:20	8
11:37	72
12:8–9	14
12:16–21	57
12:32	97
12:36–8	17
12:51–3	23
13:1–5	17
13:3, 5	21
13:20	9
14:1–24	72
14:1	72
14:12–24	12
14:12–14	89
14:13, 21	75, 113
14:26	23
14:33	23
15:1–2	62
15:3–7	98
15:11–32	21
15:17–19	19
15:18–20	22
15:31	71
16:1–8a	17
16:19–31	57
17:3–4	85
17:4	19
17:14	83
17:19	28
18:10–14	21
18:11–12	76
18:13–14	76
18:13	19, 22
18:14	71, 110
19:1–9	21
19:5–8	85
19:7	62
19:8	22, 51
19:9	22
22:18	103
22:20	99
22:29–30	97
22:35–8, 50	46

23:2	46
24:30–1, 35	72

John
2:19	103
3:22, 26	112
4:2	112
4:21–4	104
4:22	117
4:27	82
6:15	47
10:1–30	98
11	109
13:23	108
18:36	47
19:26	108
19:38	109
20:2	108

Acts
1–2	93
1:23	108
2:38	123
6:14	103
7:38	102
8:16	123
10:10–14	73
10:36	36
10:48	123
11:5–8	73
12:17	96
14:22	117
21:18	96
22:3	47

Romans
1:5	27
2:12–14	66
3:23	63
4	26
4:18	26
8:15–17	119
8:17	117
8:29	119
11:17–24	118

1 Corinthians
1:12–15	123
3:16	104

9:20–1   66
11:23–5   99
11:25   99
12   120
15:1   36
Galatians
1:14   47
2:9, 12   96
2:15   67
Ephesians
2:12   66
2:19–22   104
1 Thessalonians
4:15–17   118
Hebrews
11:8–12   26
11:11   26
11:17–18   27
James
1:1   96
2:21–2   27
1 Peter
2:5   104
1 John
3:11–18   119
Revelation
7:4–8   96
21:22   104
22:2   96

Apocrypha and Apocalyptic Books

Tobit
1:10–12   73
Judith
12:1–4, 19   73
1 Maccabees
1:60–3   68
1:62–3   73
7:5   67
9:23, 58, 69   67
11:25   67
Jubilees
2:26–31   78
50:8–9,
12–13   78–9
Psalms of Solomon
17:44–5   99

Dead Sea Scrolls

Community Rule (1QS)
6   75
a2:3–9   113
Damascus Document (CD)
10–11   79